ABG Blood Gases Made Easy

What You Will Learn From This Book:

What are the various components of a blood gas report

How to use these components and their pitfalls

Step by step approach to interpreting a blood gas report

How to confirm the given blood gas report is correct

PaO_2, SaO_2, CaO_2, Pulse oximetry

Answers to many more questions you always wanted to know

And much more

ABG Blood Gases Made Easy

Dr. A. B. Anup, MD

MBBS, MD (IM - INDIA)
DBM, DBA, MRCP (IM - UK)
BC (IM - USA), BC (MC - USA)

PUBLISHING FOR ONE WORLD

NEW AGE INTERNATIONAL (P) LIMITED, PUBLISHERS
(formerly Wiley Eastern Limited)

New Delhi • Bangalore • Chennai • Cochin • Guwahati • Hyderabad
Jalandhar • Kolkata • Lucknow • Mumbai • Ranchi
Visit us at **www.newagepublishers.com**

Disclaimer

Every effort has been made to ensure that the information in this book is as accurate and as up to date as possible. However, for the sake of simplicity some topics are oversimplified. You are recommended to consult a text book for further explanations.

Neither the author, nor the publisher, nor the editor can accept any legal responsibility for an error or omission that may have occurred.

Published by New Age International (P) Ltd., Publishers
First Edition: 2007

ISBN : 978-81-224-2113-2

Rs. 150.00

C-07-04-1481

Printed in India at Chaman Offset, Delhi
Typeset in-house

PUBLISHING FOR ONE WORLD

NEW AGE INTERNATIONAL (P) LIMITED, PUBLISHERS
(formerly Wiley Eastern Limited)
4835/24, Ansari Road, Daryaganj, New Delhi - 110002
Visit us at **www.newagepublishers.com**

Guru Govind Dono Khade
Koke Laagun Paai

Balihaari Guru Aapne
Govind Diyo Bataay
Sant Kabir

My teacher and my Lord
Stand before me
Who should I bow to first
Thanks to my teacher
Who gave me the wisdom
To know the Lord
Sant Kabir

My Deepest Regards To

All my teachers at

St. Paul's H.S. School, Ajmer, India

J.L.N Medical College, Ajmer, India

Buckland Hospital, Dover, UK

Long Island College Hospital, New York, USA

Personal Thanks

Dear Reader,

Life is a journey where you meet people who help you become a better human being. I was fortunate to know some such wonderful people in my lifetime.

A salute to my father who encouraged me to be innovative and enterprising and to my mother who imbibed in me the value of honest, hard work.

My heartfelt thanks to my wife Raksha for her relentless efforts, constant encouragement and support during the publication of this book. My special and personal thanks to my guide and best friend, Princess Kuki, who showed me that it is not what you get that is important but what you give that defines you. She also typed this manuscript.

Without all their help, support, guidance and advice I could not be what I am and this book could not be in your hands.

Dr. A B Anup, MD
15 February, 2007

This Book Will Be Useful To-

- Any physician or surgeon taking care of patients with a respiratory problem
- Post-Graduate residents in medicine
- Critical care residents, fellows and nurses
- Respiratory care residents, fellows and nurses
- Respiratory therapists
- Third and fourth year medical students to understand patient management
- Medical students in the first and the second year to understand respiratory physiology and pathology
- Anyone preparing for the NBME, USMLE, PLAB, MRCP (UK) exam
- Physician assistants taking care of patients with respiratory problems
- Anyone dealing with intubated patients including anesthesiologists, intensivists, pulmonologists and internists
- Paediatricians and Neonatologists

This book is especially written in simple English so that the maximum number of medical professionals in different countries can benefit from it.

How to Get The Most From This Book

Although there are books on the market concerning Arterial Blood Gases (and some will come in the future), the lack of a concise but comprehensive book on the subject has always been a complaint from my students. I have written this book to address that issue. I have tried to make it simple, short but comprehensive, easy to carry around and inexpensive enough to fit a resident's and student's budget.

At the outset, I recommend that you throw away the ABG graph that you may have as you will not be permitted to use it in any examination. Carry this book with you and refer it to as and when needed. Ultimately, learn to interpret all ABG reports without any outside help.

If you are a beginner start with chapter 1 and go chapter by chapter through the book. Before you go to section II you must read and understand section I. Even if you are a pro, I strongly recommend that you read section I in your free time.

If you like challenges in life - pick up a pencil and a paper and solve exercises A to G in section III. Each exercise (A,B,C...G) should take you less than six minutes to solve. That's how long it will take you once you have mastered this book. If you can complete section III in 45 minutes or less (without the help of the ABG graph) and score above 95 percent, you probably do not need to read this book. But, if not, I suggest you read it.

Clinically important points are highlighted and this will help when you review for exams.

There are two systems in the world to report blood gases. This is how these are related –

Value	SI* (units) in kPa	SI* Units Avg	Conversion factor (CF)	TU** Units Avg	TU** (unit) in mm of Hg
	Used in the UK and some other countrieS		SI x CF = TU	Used in the USA and some other countries	
PaO_2	11-13	**12**	7.5	**90**	80-100
$PaCO_2$	4.7 – 5.9	**5.6**	7.5	**40**	35-45

* Standard International (SI) Units in kPa
** Traditional Units (TU) in mm of Hg
Avg = Average Value

So if you get the report in SI Units use the conversion factor to convert the value of PaO_2 and $PaCO_2$ and then use this book. Following values are the same in both the systems.

pH 7.35 – 7.45 (no unit)
HCO_3 20-28 (meq/L or mmol/L)
SaO_2 90-100%

My best wishes to you.

Dr. A B Anup, MD
15 February, 2007

Contents

Section III Exercises

Section IV Summary

Abbreviations

ABG	=	Arterial blood gas
A-aDO_2	=	Alveolo-arterial oxygen gradient
BE	=	Base excess
CaO_2	=	Oxygen content of the whole blood
CHF	=	Congestive heart failure
CO	=	Carbon monoxide
CO_2	=	Carbon dioxide
COPD	=	Chronic obstructive pulmonary disease
DeoxyHb	=	Deoxyhemoglobin (reduced hemoglobin)
FiO_2	=	Fraction of oxygen in inspired air/gas
H^+	=	Hydrogen ion concentration
Hb	=	Hemoglobin
Hb-O_2	=	Hemoglobin Oxygen (dissociation curve)
HCO_3	=	Bicarbonate
O_2	=	Oxygen
Oxy Hb	=	Oxyhemoglobin
PaO_2	=	Partial pressure of oxygen in the arterial blood (Commonly, also called PO_2)
PAO_2	=	Partial pressure of oxygen in the air and in the alveolus
$PaCO_2$	=	Partial pressure of carbon dioxide in arterial blood (Commonly also called PCO_2)

P_B	=	Barometric pressure or atmospheric pressure
PiO_2	=	Partial pressure of oxygen in the inspired air
PvO_2	=	Partial pressure of oxygen in the venous blood
pH	=	Negative logarithm of hydrogen ion concentration (indicates acidity or alkalinity of the medium)
SaO_2	=	Saturation of hemoglobin in the arterial blood
SpO_2	=	Saturation of hemoglobin in the peripheral blood (i.e. Capillary blood)
VBG	=	Venous blood gas
WVP	=	Water vapor pressure

Section I

Basics of Blood Gas Analysis

Chapter 1

INTRODUCTION

HOW TO GET MAXIMUM INFORMATION FROM THE BLOOD GAS REPORT

Following is a typical arterial blood gas report:

pH / $PaCO_2$ / PaO_2 / HCO_3 / BE / SaO_2

> **Always read a blood gas report in context of the clinical picture of the patient**

In a non-emergency situation make it a habit to read the ABG in the following manner. By following this sequence you are less likely to miss the unusual conditions and will be more confident in case of an emergency.

Always read a blood gas report in context of the clinical picture of the patient: As you will see in the following pages, each numerical value of a blood gas result has a limited significance if read on its own i.e. without knowing the clinical picture. This is because of the number of confounders and variables affecting each parameter of the report. Most institutions use instruments that give the ABG report printouts without the patients' names and therefore errors in ABG reporting do occur sometimes. (The author knows of incidences where patients were almost intubated as the wrong blood gas report was being ascribed to them).

If the ABG report does not make sense, do not hesitate to repeat it or to get help from your seniors or colleagues. The implications of wrong treatment because of a wrong ABG report can be disastrous for the patient and may be difficult to correct later on.

Read What Is Obvious On The ABG Report:

Number 1. - SaO_2 (Saturation of the hemoglobin by oxygen)

Number 2. - HCO_3 and BE (Bicarbonate and Base Excess)

Number 3. - PaO_2 (Partial pressure of O_2 in blood. Also called PO_2)

Number 4. - $PaCO_2$ (Partial pressure of CO_2 in blood. Also called PCO_2)

Number 5. - pH

Read What Is Not Obvious On The ABG Report:

Number 6. - A-aDO_2 (A-a gradient or alveolo-arterial oxygen gradient).

Clinically, in an ABG report pH, $PaCO_2$, PaO_2 and A-aDO_2 are the most important parameters. We will see this in the following pages.

Chapter 2

SaO_2 v/s PaO_2

SaO_2: Oxygen Saturation of the Hemoglobin.

Always compare SaO_2 with the PaO_2. See Hb-O_2 dissociation curve in Chapter 3. Following are clinically important corresponding points:

PaO_2	*SaO_2**	*Clinical Importance*
40	75	Normal venous PO_2 (PvO_2)
55	88	Indication for home oxygen therapy
59	89	Indication for home oxygen therapy in a COPD patient with complications e.g. CHF or polycythemia
60	90	Point where steep fall in partial pressure of oxygen in the plasma occurs. Every attempt must be made to maintain PaO_2 above this level to prevent tissue hypoxia
80	95	Lower end of normal range for PaO_2
100	97	Higher end of normal range for PaO_2
150	99	Theoretically maximum attainable PaO_2 breathing room air at sea level
159	99.9	Theoretically maximum attainable PaO_2 breathing dry room air (without any water vapor - see chapter 5 on PaO_2)

* This correlation is approximate.

SaO_2 on the arterial blood gas is a calculated value derived from the PaO_2

SaO_2 measures the percentage of hemoglobin in oxidized form and thus saturated with oxygen. Clinically, it is **directly measured** by pulse oximetry (see below), where emitter and receiver probes are used to determine oxidized and reduced hemoglobins.

SaO_2 on the arterial blood gas is a calculated value derived from the PaO_2: In some newer co-oximeters SaO_2 is a measured value.

PaO_2 on the other hand, is obtained by running the arterial blood on the oxygen sensitive electrode in the arterial blood gas machine.

Pulse Oximetry

Pulse oximetry tells us the percentage of hemoglobin that is saturated with oxygen SO_2

Pulse oximetry tells us what percentage of the hemoglobin is saturated with oxygen - SO_2. When it is measured in the arterial blood, it is called SaO_2. The following four principles illustrate the mechanism of pulse oximetry and its shortcomings -

1. The pulse oximeters routinely used in the hospitals have three components -
   i. A source emitting two wavelengths of light i.e. red and infrared.
   ii. A receiver receiving these lights after they have passed through a part of the human body e.g. finger or ear lobule.
   iii. A computer processing unit which processes the information received from the receiver.

2. The hemoglobin in the circulation is commonly found either in the oxidized (oxyhemoglobin / Oxy Hb) or the reduced (deoxyhemoglobin / Deoxy Hb) state. Oxyhemoglobin absorbs red light and deoxyhemoglobin infrared light.
3. When a part of human body with blood flowing through it e.g. fingertip, is placed between the emitting source and the receiver, part of the light from the emitting source is absorbed by the oxyhemoglobin (red light) and part by the deoxyhemoglobin (infrared light). The remaining light falls on the receiver.
4. The computer in the processing unit calculates the saturation as follows-

$$SaO_2 \text{ (or } SpO_2\text{)} = \frac{\text{Oxy Hb}}{\text{Oxy Hb + Deoxy Hb}} \times 100$$

Since the pulse oximeter tells about the oxygen saturation of the hemoglobin in the **peripheral** circulation, it is also called SpO_2.

Remember that -

1. The **saturation reported on the ABG report SaO_2 is a calculated value,** calculated from the PaO_2. However, in newer co-oximeters the SaO_2 can be directly measured.

> The saturation Reported on the ABG report SaO_2 is a calculated value from the PaO_2

The PaO_2, SaO_2 (calculated from the PaO_2) and the SpO_2 (as read by the pulse oximeter) may all remain normal despite severe hypoxia at the tissue level. This can happen under a few clinically important but relatively uncommon circumstances. e.g. when carboxy-hemoglobin (COHb) is present or if cyanide poisoning is present. Carboxyhemoglobin is present in blood in smokers in low concentration but higher values are seen in carbon monoxide poisoning. Carboxyhemoglobin is bright red in color and absorbs red light. It is therefore read as oxyhemoglobin by the pulse oximeter. Thus despite significant carbon monoxide poisoning, the SpO_2 values may appear normal. The correct saturation of hemoglobin by the oxygen (Oxy Hb) in such cases can be determined by using an oximeter that emits four wavelengths. Two additional wavelengths record the concentration of carboxyhemoglobin (COHb) and methemoglobin (HbM or meth Hb). Thus the computer of the oximeter now reads as follows -

$$SpO_2 = \frac{\text{OxyHb}}{\text{Oxy Hb + Deoxy Hb + COHb + Meth Hb}} \times 100$$

Example: A patient with severe carbon monoxide poisoning has 8 gm% Oxy Hb, 2 gm% deoxy Hb, 4 gm% COHb. An ordinary pulse oximeter emitting light of two wavelengths will read a saturation of 80%. This is derived as follows-

$$\frac{8}{8+2} \times 100 = \frac{8}{10} \times 100 = 80\%$$

However, a pulse oximeter emitting light with four wavelengths will read the correct saturation, which is 57%.

$$SpO_2 = \frac{8}{8+2+4} \times 100 = 57\%$$

Pulse oximeters are calibrated to read only the pulsatile wave form

MethHb is present in blood in excess either as a congenital disorder or in nitrate poisoning. It is blue in color and is read more like deoxyHb and thus interferes with the correct reading by the pulse oximeter.

However, since these conditions are not very common in day to day practice, pulse oximeters in routine clinical use emit lights of only two wavelengths i.e. red and infrared for oxyHb and deoxyHb, respectively.

2. Note, that since deoxygenated blood in venous circulation can cause problems in reading the saturation of the hemoglobin in the ARTERIAL circulation (SaO_2), the pulse oximeters are calibrated only to read the pulsatile wave form (arteries have pulsation but veins do not). This eliminates interference arising from the venous circulation in reading SpO_2. However, the same principle makes it difficult to get a proper reading of SpO_2 from patients who have poor peripheral arterial circulation because of shock. Conversely, in patients with prominent venous pulsation as in those with severe tricuspid regurgitation or in those on positive pressure breathing with high inflation pressure, it may be difficult to get a correct SpO_2 reading from the pulse oximeter.

Pulse oximeter reading is not affected by static phenomena like the amount of pigment in the skin or the thickness of the finger or the ear lobule

3. Since the pulse oximeter reads only during the wave form or pulsation, the reading is not affected by static phenomena like the amount of pigment in the skin or thickness of the finger or the ear lobule. The effect of nail polish is more related to the type and color of nail polish and varies from none to significant. In an emergency if you think that the nail polish is interfering with the reading of SpO_2 put the probe on the finger from side to side or put it on the ear lobule.

SpO_2 below 70% indicates severe hypoxia and must be corrected immediately by using whatever means that may be necessary

4. Pulse oximetry is quite reliable if the saturation of the hemoglobin is above 70 percent. Since such low SpO_2 is not permitted to last for long **(SpO_2 below 70% indicates severe hypoxia and must be corrected immediately by using whatever means that may be necessary including nasal cannula, ventimask or even by intubating the patient)** the inability of the pulse oximeters to read accurately below 70 % is not a big problem in a clinical setting.
5. Other factors interfering with a correct reading on pulse oximetry include dyshemoglobinemia, severe anemia, presence of dyes in the blood (e.g. methylene blue, indigo carmine, indocyanine green) motion artifacts and cardiac arrhythmias.

Chapter 3

HEMOGLOBIN OXYGEN DISSOCIATION CURVE

NORMAL HEMOGLOBIN OXYGEN DISSOCIATION CURVE
($Hb-O_2$ dissociation curve)

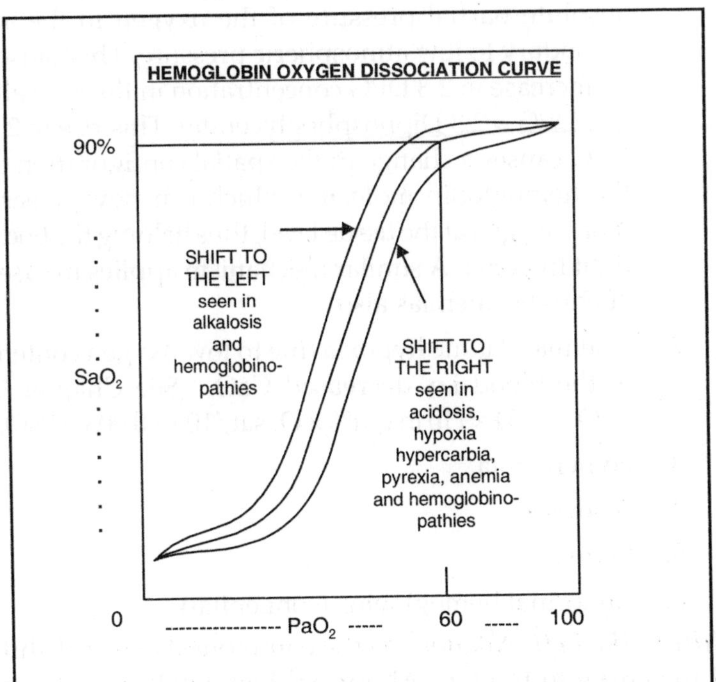

Dissociation between PaO_2 and SaO_2 could be because of many reasons.

Causes of Shift of Hemoglobin Oxygen Dissociation Curve

> In all conditions where tissue hypoxia is present, it will be the right thing for the hemoglobin-oxygen dissociation curve to shift to the right

Shift to the RIGHT: When the curve is shifted to the right the blood is able to release more oxygen in the tissues.

Therefore, in all conditions where tissue hypoxia is present, it will be the RIGHT thing for the curve to shift to the RIGHT. These conditions include:

1. High altitude causes chronic hypoxia due to low absolute partial pressure of the oxygen in the air secondary to low atmospheric pressure. This causes an increase in 2,3 DPG concentration in the red cells (2,3 DPG = 2,3 Diphosphoglycerate). This rise in 2,3 DPG causes a change in the spatial configuration of the hemoglobin molecule which can now release more oxygen at the tissue level, thus helping the body fight hypoxia. A similar mechanism applies in cases of chronic anemias also.
2. Anemia - Tissue hypoxia due to low oxygen content of the blood i.e. decreased CaO_2. (See Chapter 9: $CaO_2 = 1.34 \times \text{Hb in gm\%} \times O_2\,\text{sat}/100 + 0.003 \times PaO_2$)
3. Hypercarbia
4. Acidosis
5. Pyrexia
6. Abnormal hemoglobins (congenital)

Shift to the Left: Alkalosis is the commonest cause of shift of the curve to the left. Abnormal hemoglobin as in certain congenital hemoglobinopathies, methemoglobinemia and hereditary erythrocytosis are other important causes to remember.

Errors in the measurement of SaO_2 on the ABG: Although the error may be because of instrument malfunction, clinically important conditions like the presence of abnormal hemoglobin e.g. methemoglobin may also be responsible. Conversely, apparently normal results may be obtained in the presence of gross tissue hypoxia e. g. in the presence of carboxyhemoglobin or in cases of cyanide poisoning (see chapter on pulse oximetry)

Shifts of Hb-O_2 dissociation curve are not very significant clinically. Oxygen delivery depends on the oxygen content of the blood (See Chapter 9).

Chapter 4

HCO_3 & BE

BICARBONATE AND BASE EXCESS

HCO_3 & BE : Serum bicarbonate and Base Excess

In a blood gas report, these are calculated values derived from the pH and $PaCO_2$ by the Henderson-Hasselbalch Equation -

$$pH = \text{Constant K} \times \frac{\log HCO_3}{\log H_2CO_3}$$

Thus, the HCO_3 on the ABG report is the expected (and not directly measured) HCO_3 for that given pH and $PaCO_2$. In other words if the two values are given, the third one can be derived. That is what is done by the ABG machine which calculates the value of the HCO_3 from the values of the pH and the $PaCO_2$.

HCO_3 on the serum chemistry profile is a more accurate measure of the **ACTUAL** HCO_3 because it is directly measured. Usually HCO_3 on the ABG is slightly lower than the HCO_3 on the serum chemistry profile as the bicarbonate estimation on serum chemistry profile also includes estimation of the dissolved CO_2 in the plasma (in addition to the direct measurement of the actual bicarbonate in the serum).

$$CO_2 + H_2O \leftrightarrow H_2CO_3 \leftrightarrow H^+ + HCO_3^-$$

BASE EXCESS:

Similarly, base excess on an ABG report is a calculated value and is not used very often for routine blood gas interpretation. This may be used to evaluate total body base excess or base deficit.

Chapter 5

PaO_2

PARTIAL PRESSURE OF OXYGEN IN THE PLASMA

PaO_2: Partial pressure of oxygen: Also called PO_2. (Also see chapter 8 on A-a Gradient and 9 on CaO_2).

One very important point to remember is that PaO_2 is the **partial pressure of oxygen in the PLASMA AND NOT IN THE WHOLE BLOOD**. Although this pressure determines the saturation of the hemoglobin in most circumstances they are **NOT INTERCHANGEABLE.**

> PaO_2 is the partial pressure of oxygen in the plasma and not in the whole blood

PaO_2 is the measure of dissolved oxygen in the plasma and is dependent on the pressure (P) at which the air is being inhaled and on the fraction of oxygen in the inspired air, FiO_2. This fact is used in the treatment of patients with carbon monoxide (CO) poisoning. In cases of carbon monoxide poisoning presence of carboxyhemoglobin prevents the hemoglobin from binding with oxygen, thus causing tissue hypoxia (see chapter 9 – Section on Carbon Monoxide Poisoning).

In cases of carbon-monoxide poisoning high concentrations of oxygen is used without (mild cases) or with (severe cases) high atmospheric pressures to increase the amount of oxygen dissolved in plasma. This dissolved oxygen is then delivered to the tissue (see chapter 9 on relation of PaO_2, SaO_2 and CaO_2). Thus, inability of the hemoglobin to carry oxygen is bypassed by increasing the amount of O_2 dissolved in the plasma.

Putting it as a picture in very simple terms:

BLOOD, PaO_2 and SaO_2

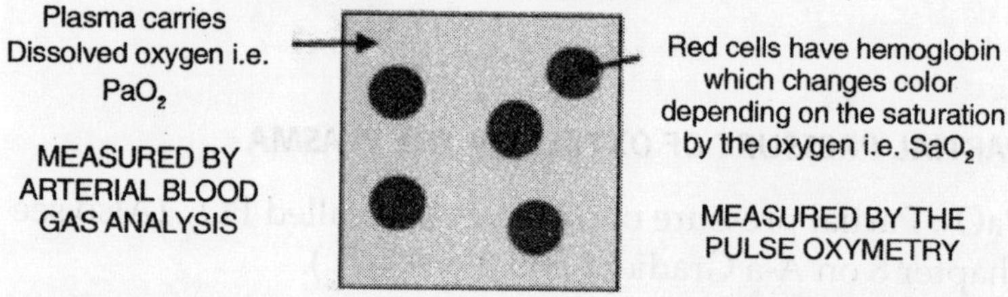

Once this fundamental is clear we can go ahead and ask, "If PaO_2 supplies only about 0.3 ml of oxygen out of up to 5 ml needed by the tissue (see chapter 9 on O_2 content of the blood) then why do we measure it and rely on it for managing patients?" The answer is simple - In most cases the PaO_2 corresponds with the hemoglobin saturation (in accordance to the Hb-O_2 dissociation curve) and therefore once we are aware of the pitfalls of the PaO_2 value we can use it.

As mentioned in chapter one **"ALL BLOOD GAS VALUES MUST BE READ IN CONTEXT OF THE CLINICAL PICTURE OF THE PATIENT"**, a patient may be severely hypoxic at the tissue level and die despite a 'normal PaO_2 value' e.g. cyanide poisoning or carbon monoxide poisoning. The point about clinical correlation can not be overemphasized.

> **Low PaO_2 indicates hypoxia**

The significance of PaO_2 is that it indicates hypoxia and since the tissues, especially the brain, cannot tolerate hypoxia for long without sustaining permanent damage, a low PaO_2 must always be corrected immediately. Depending on the severity of the hypoxia, the fraction of the oxygen in the inspired air (FiO_2) should be raised by nasal prongs/ ventimask or nonrebreather mask. The patient may even be intubated to achieve a satisfactory PaO_2. Whatever means is used, the bottom line is that a satisfactory PaO_2 should be maintained to prevent hypoxia associated injury to the tissue, especially the brain.

Normally we breathe because of a 'hypercarbic drive'.

> Cases of COPD may have response to hypercarbia blunted and breathe by the hypoxic drive

Many patients with chronic obstructive pulmonary disease (COPD) have a tendency to retain carbon dioxide and may have their respiratory center response to hypercarbia blunted. They breathe because of their 'hypoxic drive'. In such patients, **if this hypoxic drive is suddenly removed by the rapid correction of the hypoxia, then respiratory depression and even respiratory arrest can occur. In these patients one must start with lower oxygen concentration and increase the fractional inspired oxygen (FiO_2) gradually depending on the response on the patient's breathing pattern, the PaO_2 and the $PaCO_2$.**

> In some cases of COPD sudden correction of hypoxia by giving high concentrations of oxygen can lead to respiratory failure and arrest due to removal of the hypoxic drive

Beware of the following clinical situations while interpreting PaO_2

> The best way to decide whether the given sample is arterial is to know that the sample flowed freely and passively into the syringe

A. If the blood sample is a venous sample then the PaO_2 will be around 40 and $PaCO_2$ around 45 with the blood pH around 7.35. However, an identical value may be obtained on blood gas analysis if the tissue hypoxia is severe. **Remember, the best way to decide whether the given sample is arterial is to know that the sample has flowed freely and passively into the syringe** and at no time the piston was withdrawn actively. Rarely, even this criterion does not hold true!

B. If there is an air-bubble in the syringe in which the blood is drawn for the ABG, the result of the PaO_2 will be higher than the true PaO_2 of the blood (PO_2 in the air bubble is equivalent to the atmospheric pressure x FiO_2 = 760 – 47 × 0.21 = 150 where 47 is the water vapor pressure).

C. If there is a high number of WBCs (white blood cells) in the blood and the blood is made to stand for sometime before the ABG study is done, then the PaO_2 value will be lower than the true PaO_2 as the oxygen in the plasma will be consumed by those excessive WBCs to run their metabolic machinery.

D. Maximum possible PaO_2 while breathing "Room Air" is 150. Here is how it is derived:

Partial pressure of a gas = Atmospheric pressure x Fraction of that gas in the atmosphere

Oxygen forms 21 percent of the air we breathe. Thus, the FO_2 in air is 0.21.

$$\text{Partial pressure of oxygen in inspired air} = \text{Atmospheric pressure (Dry)} \times FiO_2$$

At the sea level the atmospheric pressure is 760 and the water vapor pressure is 47. Therefore, the atmospheric pressure of the dry air is 713.

Thus, $PaO_2 = (760 - 47) \times 0.21 = 713 \times 0.21 = 150$

Therefore, even if there is no hindrance to oxygen transfer across the alveolo-capillary membrane the maximum obtainable PaO_2 can not exceed 150 while breathing 'Room Air' at the sea level (where water vapor pressure is 47). Here, it is presumed that there is no ventilation perfusion mismatch. In real life there is always some ventilation perfusion mismatch under normal circumstances (see dead space ventilation). Because of this fact the PaO_2 attained while breathing room air is always below 150 (when we breathe normally it is around 100 and is increased when someone hyperventilates as during a prolonged painful attempt of arterial puncture. However, as mentioned above, it can not exceed 150).

If any PaO_2 is reported as more than 150 then it was not drawn with the patient breathing room air

Thus, if any PaO_2 is reported as more than 150, then it was not drawn with the patient breathing room air and some effect of higher concentration of FiO_2 (common scenario) or higher atmospheric pressure (extremely rare in real practice but very important to understand the calculation of PaO_2 and A-a DO_2 A-a gradient) may be responsible and should be looked for.

Some Important Situations

Theoretically speaking, if the patient is breathing 'Dry' air with no water vapor the maximally attainable PaO_2 at the atmospheric pressure will be $760 \times 0.21 = 159.6$. If this dry air is being inhaled at two times atmospheric pressure e.g. in hyperbaric chamber, the maximally attainable PAO_2 will be 319 ($2 \times 760 \times 0.21 = 319$).

Similarly, if someone is breathing 100% O_2 e.g. a ventilated patient, without any humidification and there is (theoretically) no ventilation perfusion mismatch and no humidification of the inhaled gas in the patient's airways; then the maximal attainable PiO_2 will be $(760 - 0) \times 1.0 = 760$. Maximal attainable PaO_2 (artery) can not exceed PAO_2 (alveolus). In real life because of the humidification of the inspired air, dead space ventilation, perfusion of non aerated alveoli and the hindrance provided by the alveolo-capillary membrane such PaO_2 values are not achieved.

With the above concept it is easy to understand why there is relative hypoxemia at higher altitude where the atmospheric pressure is low. For example: at a height where the atmospheric pressure is half normal i.e. $760/2 = 380$, the maximally attainable PiO_2 (Partial pressure of the inspired oxygen will be $380 \times 0.21 = 79.8$. As a result the maximally attainable PaO_2 will be less than 79.8 as the PaO_2 can not exceed PiO_2.

Since the PaO_2 keeps decreasing as we go higher and higher, mountain climbers need supplemental oxygen and aircraft need to be pressurized

Since, the PiO_2 keeps decreasing as we go higher and higher, mountain climbers need supplemental oxygen and aircraft need to be pressurized.

Exercise A: Calculate the maximal possible PaO_2 at a height where the atmospheric pressure is 75% of normal and the patient is breathing dry air.

Answer:

Maximum possible PaO_2 = Maximal possible PAO_2

At 75% atmospheric pressure partial pressure of oxygen in inhaled air (PiO_2) will be -

$$(760 \times 75/100 - 0) \times 0.21 = 120$$

Here, other variables like water vapor pressure, $PaCO_2$, dead space ventilation, V/Q mismatch etc. are considered to be 0.

Exercise B: Calculate the maximal possible PaO_2 for an intubated patient breathing 40% oxygen at 1.2 atmospheric pressure.

Answer:

Here, the FiO_2 is 0.4

Maximum possible PaO_2 = Maximal possible PiO_2

At 1.2 atmospheric pressure partial pressure of oxygen in inhaled air (PiO_2) will be -

$$[(760 \times 1.2) - 0] \times 0.4 = 912 \times 0.4 = 364.8$$

Here, other variables like water vapor pressure, $PaCO_2$, dead space ventilation, V/Q mismatch etc. are considered to be 0.

Important Oxygen Related Terms

Term	*Explanation*
FiO_2	Fraction of inspired air that is oxygen. Normal room air has FiO_2 of 0.21 (Air has 21% oxygen in it). See Chapter 9.
PAO_2	Partial pressure of oxygen in alveolar air (Considering there is no dead space ventilation and effect of PCO_2 it can be the same as PiO_2). See Chapter 5.
PiO_2	Partial pressure of oxygen in inspired air (150 at sea level and NOT dry air). See Chapter 5.
PaO_2	Partial pressure of oxygen in the arterial blood (approximately 100) – See chapter 5.
SaO_2	Percentage saturation of hemoglobin by oxygen (usually 99%) – See Chapter 2.
CaO_2	Oxygen content of blood. Total of oxygen carried with hemoglobin (approximately 18 ml) plus oxygen carried dissolved in plasma (approximately 0.3 ml). See Chapter 9.

Chapter 6

$PaCO_2$

$PaCO_2$: PARTIAL PRESSURE OF CARBON DIOXIDE (COMMONLY CALLED PCO_2)

$PaCO_2$ represents partial pressure of carbon dioxide in the arterial blood. $PaCO_2$ indicates the patient's ventilation in relation to the CO_2 produced by the body. Since under most circumstances the CO_2 production remains constant; $PaCO_2$ simply reflects the patient's ventilation status.

Normal act of breathing includes -

> $PaCO_2$ is increased in conditions where the respiratory movements do not result into good flow of air into and out of the lungs (hypoventilation)

(i) Respiratory cycle is initiated in the respiratory center of the reticular activating system in the brain stem and then traverses in the spinal cord.

(ii) The impulse to inhale travels in intercostal and phrenic nerves to neuromuscular junctions where membrane depolarization leads to muscular contraction of intercostal muscles and the diaphragm.

(iii) As a result of muscular contraction during inspiration the diaphragm moves down (increasing the size of the chest cavity vertically) and contraction of the intercostal muscles make the ribs more horizontal (increasing the antero posterior diameter of the chest).

> Type I respiratory failure has ONE problem 'hypoxia' or low oxygen levels in blood (PaO_2)

Any condition which interferes with the above mechanism leads to hypoventilation which manifests as a rise in $PaCO_2$ on the blood gas analysis. **$PaCO_2$ is increased in conditions where the respiratory movements do not result into good flow of air into and out of the lungs - Hypoventilation**. This causes type II respiratory failure. An easy way to remember associated ABG abnormalities is that **type II respiratory failure has two types of abnormalities -**

(1) Hypoxia (low PaO_2)
(2) Hypercarbia (high $PaCO_2$)

> Type II respiratory failure has TWO problems 'hypoxia' or low oxygen levels in blood (PaO_2) and 'hypercarbia' or high $PaCO_2$

Compare this with **type I respiratory failure which has only one abnormality** - Hypoxia (Low PaO_2).

Causes of hypoventilation or high $PaCO_2$

(i) Hypoventilation may be due to a weak central respiratory drive secondary to sedative or narcotic drug overdose (any central nervous depressant) or due to a head injury, raised intracranial pressure or cerebrovascular accident. It may also be due to blunting of the respiratory center's sensitivity to increased $PaCO_2$ as is seen in patients with chronic obstructive pulmonary disease (COPD).

> Patients with COPD should be given oxygen very carefully and in lower concentration with a constant watch on their breathing pattern, PaO_2 and $PaCO_2$.

Normally, a rise in the $PaCO_2$ should stimulate respiration to wash off this extra CO_2. This increased respiratory activity is mediated through the respiratory centers in the brain stem. In cases of COPD, a rise in $PaCO_2$ fails to stimulate the respiration. In these patients the respiratory drive is maintained by the hypoxia and if this hypoxia is suddenly corrected the drive to breathe is lost and respiratory failure is precipitated. To avoid this complication, **patients with COPD should be given oxygen very carefully and in lower concentration with a constant watch on their breathing pattern, PaO_2 and $PaCO_2$.**

(ii) Hypoventilation could also be because the impulse generated in the brainstem cannot reach the muscles of breathing -

- As in cervical cord injury
- Radiculopathy - a common clinical example is Guillain-Barre′ syndrome
- Nerve problem as in bilateral phrenic nerve paralysis
- Lower motor neuron involvement as in cases of late stages of motor neuron disease
- Neuromuscular junction disorder as in myasthenia gravis
- Muscle disease as in late myopathies
- Fatigue of the respiratory muscles as in late stages of asthma can also lead to alveolar hypoventilation and an increase in $PaCO_2$.

(iii) Despite intact neuromuscular pathways the thoracic cage may be so deformed that effective air flow in and out of the lungs cannot occur. This occurs in severe kyphoscoliosis in the thoracic area. A relatively fixed chest wall as can occur in advanced ankylosing spondylitis can also cause hypoventilation and a rise in the $PaCO_2$.

Similarly a thick eschar of a chest burn encasing the chest wall will lead to hypoventilation by physically limiting the expansion of the chest. Hypoventilation thus induced can be cured by escarotomy - splitting the scar surgically.

Causes of hyperventilation

$PaCO_2$ is decreased in conditions associated with hyperventilation and is seen in the following clinical situations -

- Anxiety disorder
- Painful blood collection
- Pulmonary embolism
- Early stages of an attack of asthma
- Early pneumonia
- Ventilator malfunction
- Pregnant females

> **A person may be breathing at a fast rate but may still be hypoventilating in terms of carbon dioxide produced in the body**

In pulmonary embolism, pneumonia and asthma the hyperventilation may be secondary to the stimulation of receptors in the lung or may be due to mild hypoxemia associated with these conditions. This hyperventilation tends to correct the hypoxemia and therefore these conditions may or may not show a decrease in

PaO_2 (they usually do). On the other hand hyperventilation associated with anxiety is associated with either normal or a mild increase in the PaO_2.

Remember, in cases of respiratory acidosis a high $PaCO_2$ indicates hypoventilation in relation to CO_2 produced in the body, even though the patient may appear to be breathing normally.

As mentioned earlier the $PaCO_2$ tells about total ventilation in relation to the CO_2 produced. Thus, a patient may have high $PaCO_2$ and therefore hypoventilation, despite a respiratory rate of say thirty. This can occur if the ventilatory effort is not strong enough or for any other reason the air can not be moved in and out of the lungs.

Respiratory rate alone does not always correlate with the values of the $PaCO_2$

On the other extreme a relatively smaller patient may be hyperventilating even if ventilating at the rate of say ten if the ventilator tidal volume is set too high for him.

Thus, it is important to understand and remember that **respiratory rate alone does not always correlate with the $PaCO_2$ values (hypo or hyper ventilation in terms of the carbon dioxide produced in the body).**

Chapter 7

The pH

pH is defined as negative logarithm of the hydrogen ion concentration. We will come back to this concept later in this chapter. pH indicates the acidity or alkalinity of a medium.

> **Normal blood pH varies from 7.35 to 7.45. Death is imminent at pH of below 6.9 or above 7.9**

> **Like any other component of the ABG pH must be read in the clinical context**

Normal arterial blood pH varies from 7.35 to 7.45. Death is imminent at pH of below 6.9 or above 7.9. It must be remembered that the pH, like any other component of the ABG must be read in the clinical context. For example - a patient may have a pH of 7.2 secondary to a chronic respiratory problem without the need for artificial ventilation; the same pH if occurs because of acute respiratory failure may need immediate artificial ventilation. Similarly, in the post-ictal state (post-seizure) the pH of the arterial blood may be quite low e.g. 7.0 but usually does not need intubation or ventilation as it is rapidly corrected on its own once the seizure is over and normal respiratory activity is reestablished. Thus, although there is no magic number below or above which any certain type of therapy is indicated in all cases, definitive therapy is indicated at a pH below 7.15 or above 7.6. Again, it is the overall clinical picture which decides the next best step for the management of the patient.

pH as mentioned above is the negative logarithm of the hydrogen ion concentration in the blood. Thus, a small change in the pH indicates a significant change in the hydrogen ion concentration. For example, a pH change from 7.4 to 7.1 indicates doubling of the hydrogen ion concentration from 40 to 80 nmol/L.

Acidosis is the process which either adds acid or removes alkali from the body fluids. This leads to a state of plasma called 'Acidemia'. Alkalosis is the reverse of that. Thus, alkalosis either adds alkali or removes acid from the body fluids and thus results into 'Alkalemia'. For practical purposes we have used the terms acidosis and alkalosis (rather than acidemia and alkalemia) as they are the terms used commonly in daily practice.

The concept of hydrogen ion concentration rather than the pH is gaining more and more importance and is therefore explained here in detail. One advantage of knowing the H^+ concentration is that the validity of the ABG report can be checked (see below).

pH v/s hydrogen ion concentration (H^+)

An easy formula to remember the relationship between the pH and the Hydrogen ion concentration is -

Change in pH by 0.1 = Change in hydrogen ion concentration by 20%

For example

pH	*H^+ concentration (nmol/dL)*
7.0	**100**
7.1	80
7.2	64
7.3	50
7.4	**40**
7.5	30
7.6	24
7.7	20

Thus, a pH decrease of 0.1 causes the hydrogen ion concentration to increase by 20% and an increase of the pH by 0.1 causes them to decrease by 20%. Note that in the above table 20, 24, 30, 40, 50, 64, 80 and 100 are 20 percent higher or lower from the value before or after them.

According to Henderson-Hasselbalch equation -

$$H^+ \text{ ion conc} = \text{constant K} \times \frac{PaCO_2}{HCO_3} \quad \text{(Constant K has a fixed value of 24)}$$

$PaCO_2$ of	*HCO_3 of*	*H^+ will be*	*Calculation for H^+*	*Approximate pH (See table above)*
40	24	40	24x40/24=40	7.4
60	24	60	24x60/24=60	7.2
20	24	20	24x20/24=20	7.7
40	16	60	24x40/16=60	7.2
60	16	90	24x60/16=90	7.05
20	16	30	24x20/16=30	7.5

If the $PaCO_2$, HCO_3, H^+ do not have the above relationship the blood gas report is not correct and should be repeated. This is an easy way to check the validity of the given blood gas report.

Chapter 8

Alveolo-Arterial Oxygen Gradient A-a DO_2 or A-a Gradient

A-a DO_2 is commonly called A-a gradient.

Theoretically speaking if there was no barrier to the transport of oxygen from the alveolus to the blood, the maximum PaO_2 that could be attained breathing room air will be 150 as that is the partial pressure of oxygen in the inspired air (PiO_2).

PiO_2	=	Atmospheric pressure in mm of Hg (Normal value 760)	–	Water vapor pressure at sea level (Normal 47)	×	FiO_2 (Normal 0.21)

$$PiO_2 = (760 - 47) \times 0.21 = 713 \times 0.21 = 150$$

However, in real life PaO_2 of 150 cannot be achieved as the following factors play a role:

(i) Alveolar membrane offers some resistance to the transfer of the oxygen from the alveolar space to the blood. This becomes important in conditions where this membrane is damaged or is thickened e.g. pulmonary fibrosis or pulmonary edema.

(ii) There is some CO_2 in the blood which exerts its partial pressure. Therefore PaO_2 that is equal to PAO_2 can not be achieved. The gradient (A-a Gradient) between the partial pressure of the oxygen in the alveolar space (PAO_2) and the blood (PaO_2) along with the role of $PaCO_2$ is summarized as follows -

$$A\text{-}aDO_2 = PAO_2 - PaO_2 - 1.25\ PaCO_2$$

Note that 1.25 $PaCO_2$ can also be written as –

$$PaCO_2 + 0.25\ PaCO_2$$

or still simpler form will be

$$1.25\ PaCO_2 = PaCO_2 + \frac{PaCO_2}{4}$$

Thus $A\text{-}aDO_2 = PAO_2 - PaO_2 - PaCO_2 - \frac{PaCO_2}{4}$

If you remember this formula you can calculate the alveolo arterial oxygen gradient (A-aDO$_2$) without using a pen or a calculator. That's how I do it!

In all exams, including the boards, help from calculators and graphs is prohibited. **This also applies to the graph for the reading of the ABGs!**

Example:

ABG on room air: pH 7.40 / $PaCO_2$ 40 / PaO_2 90

$A\text{-}a\ DO_2 = 150 - 90 - 40 - 40/4 = 150 - 90 - 40 - 10 = 10$

3. Ideally all the alveolar units that have blood supply should be ventilated and all the alveoli that are ventilated should be perfused. Under certain physiological (upper lung alveoli are aerated more and lower lung alveoli are perfused more) and pathological conditions (either the alveolar space is obliterated or the supplying vessel is blocked) a ventilation perfusion mismatch occurs.

The alveolus is filled with pus in pneumonia, fluid in pulmonary edema, blood in pulmonary hemorrhage,

> **Mismatch between ventilation and perfusion is clinically the most important cause of abnormally high A-a gradient**

inflammatory exudate in pneumocystis pneumonia but is still being perfused normally as the blood supply to the alveolus is not effected; this unit of lung will have perfusion but no ventilation and the A-aDO_2 will increase. On the other hand there may be a patient with pulmonary embolism, the embolus causing non-perfusion of the normally aerated alveolus leading to ventilation but no perfusion. This **mismatch between ventilation and perfusion is CLINICALLY THE MOST IMPORTANT CAUSE OF ABNORMALLY HIGH A-a GRADIENT.**

Importance of calculating the A-a gradient is clear from the fact that a normal A-a gradient means that the lungs are normal and the cause for the problem lies somewhere else. Conversely, an abnormal A-a gradient indicates a problem in the lungs. Take for example a patient who has a very high $PaCO_2$ but the A-a gradient is normal. Immediately look for a problem outside the lung. Conversely, a patient where you are suspecting say narcotic overdose leading to coma - a high A-a gradient should immediately make you think of associated lung problem e. g. aspiration.

However, if any condition causes equal loss of lung parenchyma and the vasculature the A-a gradient may remain normal as there is no ventilation perfusion mismatch.

The normal value for the A-a gradient varies with age but normally is 10 to 20 mm of Hg. One easy formula to remember is -

$$A - a\,DO_2 = \frac{Age}{4} + 4$$

Thus, if a patient is 40 years old the normal A-aDO_2 is up to 14 but if he is 80 years old the upper limit for the normal value goes up to 24 and in a 100 year old up to 29.

Thus to conclude:

$$\text{A - a } DO_2 = \text{Atmospheric pressure} - \text{Water Vapor Pressure} \times FiO_2 - PaO_2 - 1.25\, PaCO_2$$

$$= (760 - 47) \times 0.21 - PaO_2 - PaCO_2 - \frac{PaCO_2}{4}$$

$$= 713 \times 0.21 - PaO_2 - PaCO_2 - \frac{PaCO_2}{4}$$

$$= 150 - PaO_2 - PaCO_2 - \frac{PaCO_2}{4}$$

Although the most important cause of abnormal A-a Gradient (A-aDO_2) is pulmonary embolism, many lung pathologies including pneumonia, pulmonary edema, pulmonary hemorrhage and many others can cause an abnormal A-a Gradient.

Now calculate theoretical A-a gradient in a patient breathing dry room air (no water vapor) at two atmospheres pressure. His PaO_2 is 200 and $PaCO_2$ is 40.

Answer:

$$\text{A -a } DO_2 = (P_B - WVP) \times FiO_2 - PaO_2 - PaCO_2 - \frac{PaCO_2}{4}$$

$$= (760 \times 2 - 0) \times 0.21 - 200 - 40 - 40/4$$

$$= (760 \times 2) \times 0.21 - 200 - 40 - 10$$

$$= 1520 \times 0.21 - 250$$

$$= 319.2 - 250$$

$$= 69.2$$

$$\text{A-a Gradient} = (P_B - WVP) \times FiO_2 - PaO_2 - PaCO_2 - PaCO_2/4$$

To summarize -

A-a Gradient at sea level breathing room air

$$= 150 - PaO_2 - PaCO_2 - PaCO_2/4$$

Chapter 9

Relation Between PaO_2, SaO_2 and CaO_2

PaO_2 = partial pressure of oxygen in the blood plasma
SaO_2 = saturation of the hemoglobin in the blood
CaO_2 = oxygen content of the blood

> PaO_2 is the partial pressure of the oxygen in the plasma

As mentioned earlier PaO_2 is the partial pressure of the oxygen in the plasma and is estimated directly by the ABG machine by running the blood on the oxygen sensitive electrode. In other words when we say that PaO_2 is 90 we mean that the oxygen is exerting a partial pressure of 90 mm of Hg in that patient's plasma.

> SaO_2 on the blood gas report is a calculated value

Depending on the position of SaO_2 in relation to the PaO_2 on the hemoglobin - Oxygen dissociation curve, the PaO_2 value determines to what extent the hemoglobin gets saturated/oxidized by the oxygen i.e. SaO_2. SaO_2 can be obtained directly by the pulse oximeter. On a blood gas report it is a calculated value that is derived by a simple mathematical calculation from the PaO_2 value. Both these methods have shortcomings which should be appreciated (See Chapter 2 on PaO_2 and pulse oximetry).

CaO_2 is the total amount of oxygen carried by the blood including that with hemoglobin and the plasma

CaO_2 is the total amount of oxygen carried by the blood. It is calculated by the following formula:

Total Oxygen carried in the blood	=	**Oxygen carried by the hemoglobin**	+	**Oxygen carried by the plasma**

$$CaO_2 = (Hb \times 1.34 \times SaO_2) + 0.003 \times PaO_2$$

A normal person has Hb of 14 gm%, SaO2 of 99 % and PaO_2 of 100. What is the total oxygen carried by the blood in this patient?

The oxygen carried by the hemoglobin in such a case will be –

$$14 \times 1.34 \times 0.99 = 18.57 \text{ ml (in the hemoglobin)}$$

The oxygen carried dissolved in the plasma will be -

$$0.003 \times 100 = 0.3 \text{ ml only (in the plasma)}$$

Thus, $CaO_2 = 18.57 + 0.3 = 18.87$ ml

Thus, a major portion of oxygen to be supplied to the tissues is carried by the hemoglobin (98%) and only 2% by the plasma.

Under certain circumstances the oxygen carried in the plasma can be increased several fold and this property is used in the treatment of carbon monoxide poisoning.

Carbon monoxide poisoning, Hyperbaric Oxygen therapy and Oxygen content of the blood

Carbon monoxide is generated when a carbon containing substance burns in the absence of sufficient oxygen. In the blood the carbon monoxide (CO) combines with the hemoglobin forming carboxyhemoglobin (COHb). The binding of the carbon monoxide to the hemoglobin is almost two hundred times stronger than oxygen. This binding also shifts the hemoglobin oxygen dissociation curve to the left thereby decreasing oxygen release at the cellular level. This is in addition to the hypoxia caused due to a loss of binding site for oxygen on the hemoglobin molecule. Both these lead to hypoxia at the cellular level resulting into anaerobic metabolism and lactic acidosis.

Although minimal elevation in carbon monoxide in the blood occurs in smokers, toxic exposure occurs when coal, petroleum or wood (all rich in carbon) burn in an environment lacking enough oxygen. This is an important and common poisoning; especially in the elderly in the winter season. Deaths have occurred by exposure in small garages when the car engine is left running in the absence of ventilation or even when carbon monoxide has leaked into the passenger compartment of the car from the exhaust system.

One important clue to the poisoning comes from history of headache and symptoms of cold like running nose starting in many family members SIMULTANEOUSLY.

If carbon monoxide poisoning is suspected routine pulse oximetry should not be used to monitor the patient as it will give falsely high readings for the SaO_2 (See Chapter 2 Section on pulse oximetry).

Carbon monoxide poisoning can be mild, moderate or severe. Whereas the milder forms can be treated with inhalation of high flow oxygen by face mask (e.g. 10 L/minute), more severe forms (with neurological symptoms including altered mental status and / or cardiovascular changes like ischemia or arrhythmias or patients with high carbon monoxide levels) should be treated with intubation and ventilation with 100 percent oxygen with hyperbaric chamber.

In severe carbon monoxide poisoning hyperbaric oxygen therapy (oxygen at higher atmospheric pressures e.g. 2 or 3) must be used. Hyperbaric oxygen therapy has two advantages. It accelerates the process of dissociation of carbon monoxide from the hemoglobin; a process that would have taken many hours now gets completed in a few minutes. Equally important is the fact that that much more oxygen is now carried in the plasma and thus tissue hypoxia is prevented. We have seen earlier (Chapter 9, oxygen content of the blood) that at one atmospheric pressure plasma carries 0.3 ml of oxygen/dl (O_2 carried in plasma = $PaO_2 \times 0.003 = 100 \times 0.003 = 0.3$)

However, if the patient breathes dry 100 percent oxygen at a pressure of two atmospheres then theoretically maximum possible PaO_2 will be 1520. That is –

$$PiO_2 = (760 \times 2 - 0) \times FiO_2 = 1520 \times 1.0 = 1520.$$

If we presume all this PiO_2 can be transferred to the blood the blood PaO_2 will be 1520. At that PaO_2 the blood will be able to carry $1520 \times 0.003 = 4.56$ ml/dl of oxygen dissolved in plasma.

For the sake of simplicity in the above examples water vapor pressure, dead space ventilation and $PaCO_2$ are all considered as 0.

> **Remember always to speak of FiO_2 (Fraction of Oxygen in inspired Air) in terms of fraction of 1 and not as percentage**

Remember, always to speak of FiO_2 (fraction of oxygen in inspired air) in terms of fraction of 1 and NOT AS PERCENTAGE. Thus FiO_2 in a patient on a hundred percent oxygen is 1.0 and not 100. Also, a patient breathing room air breaths air at FiO_2 of 0.21 and not 21 percent. A patient on 50 percent ventimask has FiO_2 of 0.5 and not 50 percent.

Chapter 10

Basics of Reading an ABG Report

While evaluating an Acid Base Disorder look for the following ABG parameters -

Parameter	*Normal range*	*Mean value*
pH	7.35 - 7.45	7.40
$PaCO_2$	35 - 45	40
HCO_3	22 - 28	25

Some consider the normal range for the pH to be 7.38 to 7.42 and the normal range for $PaCO_2$ to be 38 to 42. However, all changes in the pH, $PaCO_2$ and HCO_3 should be calculated from the mean value (see above).

How to Read the ABG Report

Rule 1 : Look at the pH

1A - If the pH is less than 7.35 there is acidosis.

1B - If the pH is more than 7.45 there is alkalosis

1C - If the pH is 7.35 to 7.45 there is a :

- C1 - either a combined acid base disorder
- C2 - there is no acid base disorder
- C3 - there is complete compensation for the acid base disorder

Rule 2 : Look at the $PaCO_2$

2A - If the $PaCO_2$ is increased with acidosis there is respiratory acidosis

2B - If the $PaCO_2$ is decreased with a acidosis there is metabolic acidosis

2C - If the $PaCO_2$ is decreased with alkalosis there is respiratory alkalosis

2D - If the $PaCO_2$ is increased with alkalosis there is metabolic alkalosis

2E - If the $PaCO_2$ is 35 -45 with a normal pH there is probably no acid base disorder (see below) or there are two disorders moving the $PaCO_2$ in the opposite directions e.g. metabolic acidosis and metabolic alkalosis

Rule 3 : Look at the Change in the pH for 10 mm Change in $PaCO_2$

In acute respiratory failure, carbon dioxide accumulates. This forms carbonic acid and leads to acidosis. If the problem causing retention of CO_2 persists the body adjusts by forming and retaining HCO_3, mainly in the kidneys. This causes the pH to return **towards** normal. Thus, for a given rise in $PaCO_2$, the fall in blood pH is reduced. This is obvious below in rule 3A and 3B. Rule 3A shows that if the **pH falls by 0.07 for 10 mm rise in $PaCO_2$, it is acute respiratory acidosis**. Over time this fall in the pH is corrected by a rise in HCO_3. Thus, in chronic respiratory acidosis, for a 10 mm rise in $PaCO_2$ the pH falls by 0.03 only (Rule 3B). Any fall in the pH between 0.03 and 0.07 for 10 mm rise in $PaCO_2$ will be due either to a partially compensated respiratory acidosis or due to acute on chronic (mixed) respiratory acidosis.

Change in pH for 10 mm Change in $PaCO_2$

	RESPIRATORY		METABOLIC
	Acute	*Chronic*	*Acute or Chronic*
Acidosis	0.07 (Rule 3A)	0.03 (Rule 3B)	The two digits of the pH after the decimal are the same as the $PaCO_2$. (Rule 3E)
Alkalosis	0.08 (Rule 3C)	0.03 (Rule 3 D)	Same as above 3E (Rule 3 F)

Rule 4: Look for Change in HCO_3 for 10 mm Change in $PaCO_2$

	RESPIRATORY		METABOLIC	
	Acute	*Chronic*	*Acute*	*Chronic*
Acidosis	1-1.2 (Rule 4A)	3 - 4 (Rule 4B)	10 (Rule 4C)	10 (Rule 4D)
Alkalosis	2.5 (Rule 4E)	5.0 (Rule 4F)	14 (Rule 4G)	14 (Rule 4H)

The change in bicarbonate for a given change in pH or $PaCO_2$ tells whether there is compensation or not; and if there is compensation, whether it is appropriate and complete or not. If the compensation is not appropriate then a mixed disorder should be looked for.

The above can be summarized as follows:

pH	*Acidosis/ Alkalosis*	*$PaCO_2$*	*HCO_3*	*Disorder*
Decreased	Acidosis	Increased	Increased	**Respiratory acidosis**
Decreased	Acidosis	Decreased	Decreased	**Metabolic acidosis**
Increased	Alkalosis	Increased	Increased	**Metabolic alkalosis**
Increased	Alkalosis	Decreased	Decreased	**Respiratory alkalosis**

To simplify it further:

Since it is obvious from the above table that $PaCO_2$ and HCO_3 move in the same direction, for simple disorders the above can be summarized as follows -

$PaCO_2$ or HCO_3	*Decreased pH (Acidosis)*	*Increased pH (Alkalosis)*
Decreased	Metabolic	Respiratory
Increased	Respiratory	Metabolic

Limits of Compensation

- During respiratory acidosis, CO_2 is retained. This causes an increase in HCO_3. During acute respiratory acidosis, the HCO_3 cannot rise above 30. However, during the chronic phase of the acidosis the kidneys retain HCO_3 and it can rise up to 55.
- During respiratory alkalosis, the $PaCO_2$ falls due to hyperventilation. However, it cannot fall below 16 to 18 mm of Hg. Lower $PaCO_2$ causes an increase in pH. At higher pH tetany may occur due to a fall in fraction of ionized calcium (Alkalosis decreases the fraction of ionized calcium).
- During metabolic acidosis, deep and frequent breathing occurs, causing a fall in the $PaCO_2$. However, the $PaCO_2$ does not fall below 10 - 12 in adults and about 6 - 8 in children.
- During metabolic alkalosis, hypoventilation occurs causing an increase in $PaCO_2$. The $PaCO_2$ cannot rise above 55, as further hypoventilation is prevented by hypoxia.
- Values of HCO_3 and $PaCO_2$ beyond those described can be seen in mixed acid base disorders.
- When a disorder compensates, **there is never 'overcompensation'**. In other words if patient tries to correct for respiratory acidosis by retaining

bicarbonate, then he will never retain so much bicarbonate as to cause alkalosis.

HOW TO APPROACH AN ACID BASE DISORDER

1. Look at the pH
2. Look at the $PaCO_2$
3. Look at the HCO_3
4. Evaluate degree of compensation or correction
5. Evaluate the ABG for a mixed acid base disorder

For a stepwise approach to the ABG report please see the next page.

HOW TO APPROACH AN ACID BASE DISORDER ON THE ABG REPORT

Look at the pH
!
!----Below 7.35 --- there is acidosis
! !
! Look at the $PaCO_2$
! !
! !---Above 45 means acidosis is respiratory
! ! !
! ! !--- Look for increase in HCO_3 for
! ! ! 10 mm increase in $PaCO_2$
! ! ! - if 1 - 1.2 -- Acute respiratory acidosis
! ! ! - if 1.3 - 3 -- Partial compensation
! ! ! - if 3.1 -4 -- Full compensation
! ! !
! ! !--- Look for fall in pH for 10 mm rise in $PaCO_2$
! ! - if 0.08 -- Acute respiratory acidosis
! ! - if 0.03 -- Chronic respiratory acidosis
! !
! !--- Below 35 means acidosis is metabolic.
! In pure metabolic acidosis
! - $PaCO_2$ is the same as two digits of the pH
! After the decimal (Rule 1)
! - or $PaCO_2 = (1.5 \times HCO_3) + 8 \pm 2$ (Rule J)
! - or $PaCO_2 = HCO_3 + 15$ if HCO_3 is above 10 (Rule K)
!
!------ Above 7.45 means that there is alkalosis
! !
! Look at the $PaCO_2$
! !
! !--- Below 35 means alkalosis is respiratory
! ! !
! ! !-- look for fall in HCO_3 for 10 mm fall in $PaCO_2$
! ! ! - if 2.5 --- Acute respiratory alkalosis
! ! ! - if 5 ------ Chronic respiratory alkalosis
! ! !
! ! !-- look for rise in pH for 10 mm fall in $PaCO_2$
! ! - if 0.08 --- Acute respiratory alkalosis
! ! - if 0.03 --- Chronic respiratory alkalosis
! !--- Above 45 means alkalosis is metabolic
! Expected $PaCO_2 = 0.7 \times HCO_3 + 20 \pm 1.5$
!
!---- if 7.35 to 7.45 Possibilities can be
A) No acid base disorder
B) Compensated disorder
C) Mixed disorder

Section II

Blood Gas Interpretation

Chapter 11

Respiratory Acidosis

Ex 1 : ABG pH 7.28 $PaCO_2$ 60 HCO_3 27

Step	*Observation*	*Interpretation*
1.	pH is below 7.35	There is acidosis (Rule 1A)
2.	$PaCO_2$ is increased	Acidosis is respiratory (Rule 2A)
3.	$PaCO_2$ is increased by 20 from 40 and the HCO_3 by 2 from 25. Thus the HCO_3 rise is by 1 for 10 mm rise in $PaCO_2$	The compensation is full (Rule 4A) for acute respiratory acidosis. The HCO_3 did not have enough time to rise. Therefore, the marked fall in the pH.
4.	pH has fallen by 0.12 from 7.4 for 20 mm rise in $PaCO_2$ from a mean of 40 (0.06 for a 10 mm rise in $PaCO_2$)	This is appropriate compensation for acute respiratory acidosis (Rule 3A)

Diagnosis: Pure acute respiratory acidosis

Causes of respiratory acidosis are causes of hypoventilation (See Chapter 6 on $PaCO_2$). Note that during **acute** respiratory acidosis, for the pH to fall from 7.40 to 7.28 the $PaCO_2$ has increased from 40 to 60. For a similar fall in the pH during **chronic** respiratory acidosis, the $PaCO_2$ rises up to 80 (see exercise 2 on the next page). This relatively lesser fall in pH for given rise in $PaCO_2$ is due to a rise in the HCO_3 from 27 to 39 in chronic respiratory acidosis. This process takes a few days and helps the pH to return towards normal.

Ex 2 **:** ABG pH 7.28 $PaCO_2$ 84 HCO_3 39

Step	*Observation*	*Interpretation*
1.	pH is below 7.35	There is acidosis (Rule 1A)
2.	$PaCO_2$ is increased	Acidosis is respiratory (Rule 2A)
3.	$PaCO_2$ is increased by 44 from 40 and HCO_3 by 14 from 25. Thus the rise in HCO_3 is 3.2 for 10 mm rise in $PaCO_2$	The compensation is full (Rule 4B) for chronic respiratory acidosis. The HCO_3 has risen well so the effect on the pH is much lesser despite a very high $PaCO_2$ of 84.
4.	pH has fallen by 0.12 (from mean 7.4) for 44 mm (from 40) rise of $PaCO_2$ i.e. 0.028 for 10 mm change in $PaCO_2$	Change in pH is appropriate for it to be chronic respiratory acidosis (Rule 3B)

Diagnosis: Pure chronic respiratory acidosis.

Causes of respiratory acidosis: These are basically the causes of hypoventilation (see chapter 6 on $PaCO_2$). Note here that the HCO_3 has risen from 25 to 39 and as a result the effect on the pH has been much lesser despite a much higher $PaCO_2$ (compare ABG reports in exercise 1 and 2 above).

Chapter 12

METABOLIC ACIDOSIS

Ex 3 : ABG pH 7.30 $PaCO_2$ 30 HCO_3 15

Step	*Observation*	*Interpretation*
1.	The pH is below 7.35	There is acidosis (Rule 1A)
2.	$PaCO_2$ is decreased	Acidosis is metabolic (Rule 2B)
3.	i) $PaCO_2$ value is the same as the last two digits after the decimal in the pH (Rule 3E)	The numbers are correct for it to be pure metabolic acidosis according to rule 3E.
	ii) $HCO_3 + 15 = PaCO_2$ Here HCO_3 is 15 and $PaCO_2$ is 30.	15 + 15 = 30. Rule K (see algorithm) is satisfied.
	iii) $PaCO_2 = 1.5\ HCO_3 + 8$ Here, $1.5 \times HCO_3 + 8$ is 22.8 + 8 or 30.5 (Rule J)	Measured $PaCO_2$ is 30 and calculated 30.5. Rule J is satisfied. Therefore it is pure metabolic acidosis.

Diagnosis: Pure metabolic acidosis

As soon as you diagnose metabolic acidosis you must calculate the anion gap

Remember that **as soon as you diagnose metabolic acidosis you must calculate the anion gap.** This will immediately classify the acidosis into two classes -

1. Anion gap metabolic acidosis or **AGMA**
2. Non anion gap metabolic acidosis or **NAGMA**

The Concept of Anion Gap

It must be clear from the very beginning that **no such gap really exists in the body** (In - vivo) and this is only a concept - an **In-Vitro phenomenon** (In- vitro = outside the body).

> **Total number of anions in the body equals the total number of cations and if each and every anion and cation is accounted for, there will be no anion gap**

Normally, there are positively and negatively charged ions in our body. Positively charged ions are called **CATIONS and include Sodium, Potassium, Calcium, Magnesium, globulins** and many more including minerals and rare elements.

Negatively charged ions are called **ANIONS and include Chloride, Bicarbonate, Sulfate, Phosphate, Albumin** and other organic ions which are produced in the body as a result of metabolism.

> **In body there is no anion gap as total number of positive ions is equal in number to negative ions**

Total number of anions in the body equals the total number of cations and if each and every anion and cation is accounted for, there will be no anion gap. This, however would be very cumbersome, time consuming and financially impractical. Therefore, we only estimate the major cations and anions for calculating the anion gap. We subtract the major anions (Chloride and HCO_3, 110 and 25 meq respectively) from major cations (sodium 140 meq) and label the difference as anion gap. Thus, this **gap represents those negatively charged ions (anions) in the body which are balancing the electric charge of the positively charged ions (cations) but are not estimated** (See picture).

Thus **Anion gap = Na – Cl – HCO_3**

> Anion Gap = Na – Cl – HCO_3

Considering normal sodium of 140 meq/dl and chloride of 100 meq/dl and HCO_3 of 25, the anion gap will be –

AG = 140 – 100 – 25 = 15

> Normal Anion Gap is 12 $\pm$ 4

Normal anion gap is 12 $\pm$ 4 i.e. 8 to 16. Some consider the normal range to be 10 to 14.

In cases with **pure anion gap metabolic acidosis, the rise in anion gap from 12 should equal the fall in HCO_3 from 24.** If there is significant discrepancy then a mixed disorder should be considered. **This is the principle behind the concept of gap-gap which is expressed as a ratio of change in anion gap to the change in HCO_3.**

> Gap-Gap is the Ratio of Rise in Anion Gap to fall in HCO_3

In pure anion gap metabolic acidosis this ratio remains as one. Considering that in a patient the anion gap is 20, (increased by 8 from mean of 12) the fall in serum bicarbonate (more than or less than 8 from 25) will make the ratio above or below one. **Thus the gap-gap helps us decide about the presence of a mixed acid base disorder.**

Concept of Anion Gap

Total Cations (In body) = Total Anions (In body)

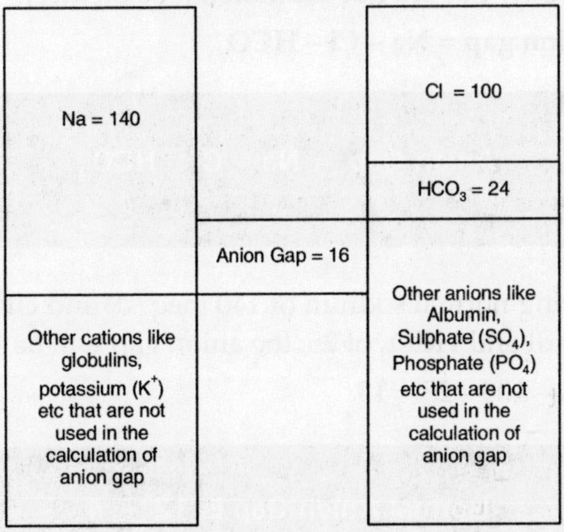

Causes of Increased Anion Gap

The anions may be added to the body and therefore to the blood, from an outside source (exogenous) or from within the body as a result of metabolism (endogenous). Although, there is a common mnemonic to remember the causes as **MUDPILES** (Methanol, Uremia, Diabetic ketoacidosis, Paraldehyde, Iron or INH, Lactic acidosis, Salicylates), it is much more important to understand the pathophysiology of the process. The above mnemonic puts less important and less common causes first. Further, more important causes are not distinguished. Also, one alphabet represents more than one important clinical disorder e.g. 'S' stands for salicylates, sepsis and starvation. **A much better mnemonic which is clinically oriented will be - 'DARLINGS ARE IMP (ortant)'.**

D	Diabetic keto-acidosis
A	Alcohol
R	Renal failure
L	Lactic acidosis from any cause
I	Iron poisoning
N	No food (starvation)
G	Generalized seizures
S	Sepsis
A	Aspirin poisoning
R	Rhabdomyolysis
E	Ethylene glycol
I	INH
M	Methanol
P	Paraldehyde

Important Endogenous Sources of Anions include

Cause	*Anion accumulated*
1. Cardiopulmonary failure	- Lactate
2. Renal failure	- Organic acids, SO_4, PO_4
3. Diabetes Mellitus	- Keto acids
4. Starvation	- Keto acids
5. Anaerobic metabolism	- Lactate

Important Exogenous Sources of Anions Include

Cause	*Anion accumulated*
1. Salicylates	- Salicylic acid
2. Ethanol	- Keto and lactic acid
3. Methanol	- Formic acid
4. Ethylene glycol	- Glycolic and oxalic acid
5. Paraldehyde	

All the above are causes of AGMA (anion gap metabolic

In all cases of high anion gap, look for measured serum osmolality and its difference from calculated serum osmolality. The difference is called the osmolal gap

acidosis). **In all cases of high anion gap, look for measured serum osmolality and its difference from calculated serum osmolality. The difference is called the osmolal gap and it is increased if the blood contains substances with osmolality different from that of plasma and if these substances are not used in calculating serum osmolality, e.g. ethanol** which has osmolality of 23 or methanol with osmolality of 34 mOsm (approximately) at 100 mg/dl blood level.

$$\text{Serum Osmolality (Calculated)} = 2 \times \text{Na} + \frac{\text{Glucose}}{18} + \frac{\text{Urea}}{2.8}$$

Measuring serum osmolality directly additionally measures osmolality imparted by other osmotically active substances such as alcohols. Therefore, measured **serum osmolality is higher than calculated serum osmolality if the patient has consumed alcohol.** The degree of increase in osmolality varies and depends on the type of alcohol in the blood. Each 100 mg% of ethanol increases osmolality by 23. Corresponding rise in osmolality by methanol and isopropyl alcohol is 34 and 16 respectively (approximately).

$$\text{Serum Osmolality (Calculated)} = 2 \times \text{Na} + \frac{\text{Glucose}}{18} + \frac{\text{Urea}}{2.8} + \text{other osmotically active substances}$$

Remember that **salicylates give an anion gap metabolic acidosis but do not increase osmolality**. On the other hand **Isopropyl alcohols increase serum osmolality but do not increase the anion gap**. Ethanol and methanol increase both the osmolality and the anion gap.

Isopropyl alcohol is the common rubbing alcohol on hospital

wards. Methanol is used as a de-icing agent in windshield fluids and ethylene glycol is used as antifreeze in cars.

Albumin is a negatively charged particle (anion). In the serum

> **When serum albumin significantly decreases the anion gap decreases too**

it counterbalances the cations (e.g. Na) but is not used as a component of negatively charged ions while calculating the total number of anions. Therefore, it is responsible (along with some other anions) for the anion gap phenomenon.

As a result **when serum albumin significantly decreases, the anion gap decreases too**. Conversely, globulins are positively charged particles (cation) and their increase (globulins) causes a decrease in the anion gap. **Sometimes, a low anion gap is the first clue to the presence of increased globulins or paraproteins (e.g. multiple myeloma) in the body.**

Always remember, as said earlier, if we measure all the

> **Sometimes, a low anion gap is the first clue to the presence of increased globulins or paraproteins (e.g. multiple myeloma) in the body**

cations and anions in the serum there will be no anion gap as all the cations will balance all the anions.

Non Anion Gap Acidosis: NAGMA

In the conditions causing NAGMA there is **acidosis, but** the balance between sodium on one side and chloride and bicarbonate on the other is not disturbed. The loss of bicarbonate is compensated by a rise in chloride. Therefore, the **anion gap (Na - Cl - HCO_3) is not changed.**

Important causes of loss of bicarbonate include:

1. Gastrointestinal losses
   - Diarrhea
   - Small bowel fistula
   - Continuous small bowel drainage
   - Ileostomy
   - Ureterosigmoidostomy
   - Ileal conduit for ureter
2. Urinary losses
   - Proximal renal tubular acidosis
   - Distal renal tubular acidosis
   - Acetazolamide therapy
   - Urinary obstruction

> **Both an anion gap acidosis and non-anion-gap acidosis may be present together in the same patient**

Sometimes, both an anion gap acidosis and non-anion-gap acidosis are present together in the same patient e.g. Diabetic ketoacidosis in a patient with renal tubular acidosis. The clue to the disorder comes from the fact that the **fall in HCO_3 is excessive for the given degree of anion gap** (both from the mean) when other causes of low HCO_3 e.g. respiratory alkalosis have been excluded. For example, if a patient has an anion gap of 18 (6 above a mean of 12) then the expected HCO_3 will be 19 (6 below mean of 25). If, however, the patient's serum HCO_3 is 12 and there is only pure metabolic acidosis; then consider the presence of both anion gap and non anion gap metabolic acidosis.

Chapter 13

RESPIRATORY ALKALOSIS

Ex 4 : ABG pH 7.54 $PaCO_2$ 25 HCO_3 21

Step	*Observation*	*Interpretation*
1.	The pH is above 7.45	There is alkalosis (Rule 1B)
2.	$PaCO_2$ is decreased	Alkalosis is respiratory (2C)
3.	$PaCO_2$ is decreased by 15 from 40 and the HCO_3 by 4 from 25. Thus the fall in HCO_3 is 2.7 for 10 mm fall in $PaCO_2$	The compensation is full (Rule 4E) for acute respiratory alkalosis. The HCO_3 did not have enough time to fall therefore the marked rise in the pH.
4.	For a 15 mm fall in $PaCO_2$ the pH has gone up by 0.14 from 7.4 i.e. a rise of pH of 0.09 for 10 mm fall in $PaCO_2$	There is appropriate compensation for pure acute respiratory alkalosis (Rule 3C)

Diagnosis:

Pure acute respiratory alkalosis.

Causes of respiratory alkalosis can be either nonpulmonary or pulmonary

Causes of respiratory alkalosis can be either nonpulmonary or pulmonary. Non pulmonary causes include hysteric hyperventilation or CNS disorders like encephalitis. Pulmonary causes include pulmonary embolism, early pneumonia and early stages of bronchial asthma.

pH that is normal or towards respiratory acidosis in a patient with a severe attack of asthma is a dangerous sign and indicates impending respiratory failure with a possible need for intubation and ventilation

Remember, **a pH that is normal or towards respiratory acidosis in a patient with a severe attack of asthma is a dangerous sign and indicates impending respiratory failure with a possible need for intubation and ventilation.** Similarly, **if in an asthmatic the initial low $PaCO_2$ on ABG is normalizing and the patient's clinical condition is getting worse then probably respiratory exhaustion is setting in causing hypoventilation and increasing the $PaCO_2$.**

Ex 5 : ABG pH 7.46 $PaCO_2$ 20 HCO_3 15

Step	*Observation*	*Interpretation*
1.	The pH is above 7.45	There is alkalosis
2.	$PaCO_2$ is decreased	Alkalosis is respiratory
3.	$PaCO_2$ is decreased by 20 from 40 and HCO_3 by 10 from 25. Thus, the fall in HCO_3 is 5 for 10 mm fall in $PaCO_2$	The compensation is full (Rule 4F) for chronic respiratory alkalosis. The HCO_3 has fallen enough; therefore, the minimal rise in the pH. Compare this with exercise 4 above.
4.	For a 20 mm fall in $PaCO_2$ the pH has gone up by 0.06 from 7.4 i.e. rise in pH of 0.03 for 10 mm fall in $PaCO_2$	There is appropriate compensation for pure chronic respiratory alkalosis (Rule 3D).

Diagnosis: Pure chronic respiratory alkalosis.

In respiratory alkalosis the compensation becomes complete in about two weeks and the pH returns **towards** normal.

The lowest $PaCO_2$ that can be achieved by hyperventilating is approximately 16.

Chapter 14

METABOLIC ALKALOSIS

Ex 6 : ABG pH 7.56 $PaCO_2$ 55 HCO_3 45

Step	*Observation*	*Interpretation*
1.	pH is above 7.45	There is alkalosis (Rule 1B)
2.	$PaCO_2$ is increased	Alkalosis is metabolic (Rule 2C)
3.	$PaCO_2$ value is the same as the last two digits of the pH after the decimal point	The compensation is full (Rule 3F) for pure metabolic alkalosis
4.	$PaCO_2$ is increased by 15 from 40 and HCO_3 by 20 from 25. Thus the rise in HCO_3 is 14 for 10 mm rise in $PaCO_2$	The compensation is full (Rule 4G/H) for metabolic alkalosis

Diagnosis: Pure metabolic alkalosis

Whenever you diagnose metabolic alkalosis look for urinary chloride to decide whether the alkalosis will respond to administration of chloride or not. **The commonest cause of metabolic alkalosis in clinical practice is diuretic therapy.** Metabolic alkalosis in these patients responds well to the stopping of the diuretic therapy. Another very common cause of metabolic alkalosis is volume contraction due to dehydration. It responds well to chloride administration (salt) orally or intravenously as saline therapy.

Causes of Metabolic Alkalosis

The commonest causes of metabolic alkalosis in clinical practice are dehydration and diuretic therapy

Common causes of metabolic alkalosis can be divided into chloride responsive and chloride resistant depending on whether the urine chloride is below or above 15 meq/L.

Chloride responsive metabolic alkalosis is associated with low urinary chloride (below 15 meq/L) and can be due to:

- Vomiting
- Continuous nasogastric suction
- Volume contraction states

Chloride resistant metabolic alkalosis is associated with urinary chloride above 15 meq/L and occurs in:

- Hypercortisolism
- Hyperaldosteronism
- Sodium bicarbonate therapy
- Severe renal artery stenosis

Exception: **The situation of metabolic alkalosis with use of diuretics is a special one.** Since they are natriuretic, diuretics increase urinary loss of sodium and chloride. However, the alkalosis induced by them responds to administration of saline. Thus, **despite a high urinary chloride the alkalosis due to diuretic therapy responds to chloride administration.**

Chapter 15

MIXED ACID BASE DISORDERS

Ex 7 : ABG pH 7.2 $PaCO_2$ 80 HCO_3 32

Step	*Observation*	*Interpretation*
1.	pH is below 7.35	There is acidosis
2.	$PaCO_2$ is increased	Acidosis is respiratory
3.	$PaCO_2$ is increased by 40 from 40 and the HCO_3 has increased by 7 from 25. Thus the rise in HCO_3 is 1.8 for 10 mm rise in $PaCO_2$	For acute respiratory acidosis HCO_3 should rise by 1 and for chronic respiratory acidosis by 3 to 4 for a 10 mm rise in $PaCO_2$ (Rule 4A,4B). A rise of 1.8 could either be due to a partial correction of an acute respiratory acidosis by compensation or may be due to acute-on-chronic respiratory acidosis.
4.	$PaCO_2$ rise of 40 is matched with a pH fall of 0.2 from 7.4 i.e. a fall in pH of 0.05 for 10 mm rise in $PaCO_2$	In acute respiratory acidosis for 10 mm rise in $PaCO_2$ the pH falls by 0.07 and in chronic phase by 0.03. Fall of 0.05 may either be due to an acute-on-chronic respiratory failure or due to incomplete (Rule 3A, 3B) compensation

Diagnosis:

Acute-on-chronic respiratory acidosis

Or

Partially compensated acute respiratory acidosis

Ex 8 : ABG pH 7.2 $PaCO_2$ 50 HCO_3 19

Step	*Observation*	*Interpretation*
1.	pH is below 7.35	There is acidosis
2.	$PaCO_2$ is increased	Acidosis is respiratory
3.	$PaCO_2$ is increased by 10 from 40 but HCO_3 is decreased. In simple disorders $PaCO_2$ and HCO_3 always move in the same direction i.e. either increased or decreased	If the disorder is pure respiratory acidosis the HCO_3 with this rise in $PaCO_2$ of ten should be 26-30 (Rule 4A/4B) but it is only 19. Thus a mixed disorder is present. On top of respiratory acidosis there is a disorder decreasing the HCO_3. It could either be metabolic acidosis or respiratory alkalosis (either of them can decrease the HCO_3)
4.	$PaCO_2$ rise of 10 is matched with pH fall of 0.2 from 7.4. If it is pure respiratory acidosis maximum fall in pH possible is 0.07. Here, the fall in pH is much more	The fall in the pH is out of proportion to expected due to respiratory acidosis. Therefore, an additional disorder causing acidosis is present which is associated with a fall in HCO_3. Metabolic acidosis fits all these criteria.

Diagnosis:

Mixed disorder with respiratory acidosis and metabolic acidosis

Ex 9 : ABG pH 7.45 $PaCO_2$ 70 HCO_3 50

Step	*Observation*	*Interpretation*
1.	pH is normal at 7.45	3 possibilities can be a) No acid base disorder b) Compensated disorder c) Mixed disorder
2.	$PaCO_2$ is increased	Possibility (a) is excluded. There is an acid base disorder (b) or (c)
3.	$PaCO_2$ is increased by 30 (70 from 40) and HCO_3 by 25 (50 from 25). Thus, for 10 mm rise in $PaCO_2$ the HCO_3 has increased by 8. $PaCO_2$ rise of 30 is associated with pH rise of 0.05 from 7.4.	If it is compensated respiratory acidosis, the HCO_3 value with this rise in $PaCO_2$ of 30 can at the most be 37 (Rule 4B) but it is 50. Thus, a mixed disorder is present. On top of respiratory acidosis there is a disorder increasing the HCO_3 and increasing the pH from acidosis to alkalotic side. Metabolic alkalosis fits all these criteria
4.	$PaCO_2$ rise of 30 is associated with pH rise of 0.05 from 7.4. If there is pure respiratory acidosis possible fall in the pH could be from 0.1 to 0.21. Here the pH has rather risen by 0.05	The change in the pH is in the opposite direction of expected due to respiratory acidosis. Therefore, an additional disorder causing alkalosis is present which is associated with a rise in HCO_3. Metabolic alkalosis fits all these criteria.

Diagnosis:

Mixed disorder with metabolic alkalosis and respiratory acidosis.

Chapter 16

MISCELLANEOUS DISORDERS

Ex 10 : ABG pH 7.35 $PaCO_2$ 50 HCO_3 28

Step	*Observation*	*Interpretation*
1.	pH is normal at 7.35	3 possibilities can be a) No acid base disorder b) Compensated disorder c) Mixed disorder
2.	$PaCO_2$ is increased	Possibility (a) is excluded. There is an acid base disorder (b) or (c).
3.	$PaCO_2$ is increased by 10 from 40 and HCO_3 by 3 from 25	If it is compensated respiratory acidosis, then with a 10 mm rise in $PaCO_2$ the HCO_3 can be 26 to 29 (acute to chronic disorder - Rule 4A, 4B). Here it is 28. Thus it is compensated respiratory acidosis.
4.	$PaCO_2$ rise of 10 is associated with pH fall of 0.05 from 7.4	The fall in the pH is as expected i.e. 0.03 to 0.07 (Rule 3A, 3B) for respiratory acidosis. There is no mismatch. Therefore this is fully compensated respiratory acidosis.

Diagnosis:

Compensated respiratory acidosis

Ex 11 : ABG pH 7.38 $PaCO_2$ 39 HCO_3 23

Step	*Observation*	*Interpretation*
1.	pH is normal at 7.38	4 possibilities are a) No acid base disorder b) Compensated disorder c) Mixed disorder d) Wrong ABG report
2.	$PaCO_2$ is normal	Probably there is no acid base disorder (Rule 2E). Also, see below.
3.	HCO_3 is normal	
4.	H^+ for a pH of 7.38 will be 42. (See chapter 7 on pH and H^+ concentration - pH of 7.3 and 7.4 correspond to a H^+ of 50 and 40 respectively).	$H^+ = \frac{24 \times PaCO_2}{HCO_3}$ OR $H^+ = \frac{24 \times 39}{23}$ (See chapter 7 on pH and H^+ concentration)

Diagnosis:

No evidence of an acid base disorder on the ABG analysis. Correlate clinically. Rare possibility of metabolic acidosis (which will decrease the pH, $PaCO_2$ and HCO_3) and metabolic alkalosis (which will increase the pH, $PaCO_2$ and HCO_3) occurring together cannot be excluded.

Ex 12 : ABG pH 7.6 $PaCO_2$ 35 HCO_3 32

Step	*Observation*	*Interpretation*
1.	pH is 7.6	There is alkalosis
2.	$PaCO_2$ is decreased 5 mm from a mean of 40	There is respiratory alkalosis (next - look for compensation).
3.	$PaCO_2$ is decreased by 5 from 40 and HCO_3 is increased by 7 from 25	If it is compensated respiratory alkalosis, HCO_3 should fall by 1.2 to 2.5 with 5 mm fall in $PaCO_2$ (Rule 4E, 4F). However, here it has risen by 7. Thus a mixed disorder is present. On top of respiratory alkalosis there is a disorder increasing the HCO_3. The other disorder that can cause such a change is metabolic alkalosis
4.	$PaCO_2$ fall of 5 is associated with a pH rise of 0.2 from 7.4. If it was pure respiratory alkalosis the rise in pH should have been 0.015 to 0.04 (Rule 3C, 3D). However, here the pH has risen by 0.2	The rise in the pH is much more than expected. Therefore an additional disorder causing a rise in the pH and rise in HCO_3 (see point 3 above) is present. Metabolic alkalosis fits all these criteria.

Diagnosis:

Mixed disorder with respiratory alkalosis and metabolic alkalosis.

Ex 13 : ABG from a healthy 24 year old female

pH 7.4 $PaCO_2$ 28 HCO_3 16

Step	*Observation*	*Interpretation*
1.	pH is 7.4	Normal pH
2.	$PaCO_2$ is decreased	3 possibilities can be a) Metabolic acidosis with respiratory alkalosis b) very early stage of hyperventilation c) wrong ABG report
3.	HCO_3 is decreased	Since it takes time to decrease the HCO_3 the second possibility is ruled out. Also note that the pH is normal.
4.	The patient is healthy	First possibility is unlikely.
5.	Is the ABG report correct? $H^+ = \frac{24 \times PaCO_2}{HCO_3}$ should hold true (see chapter 7 on pH)	Here H^+ ion concentration is ~40 (corresponds to a pH of 7.4) $H^+ = \frac{24 \times 28}{16} = 42$ The relationship holds true. Thus ABG report is correct.
6.	Go back to the clinical picture. She is a young healthy female.	Could it be that she is pregnant? In pregnancy the $PaCO_2$ decreases. This is probably due to the effect of progesterone. The pH is maintained normal by a corresponding fall in the HCO_3.

Diagnosis:

Normal ABG in a Pregnant Female

Ex 14 : ABG pH 7.5 $PaCO_2$ 20 HCO_3 22

Step	*Observation*	*Interpretation*
1.	pH is 7.5	The patient has alkalosis
2.	$PaCO_2$ is decreased	Alkalosis is respiratory
3.	For 10 mm fall in $PaCO_2$ the pH rises by 0.08 in acute and 0.03 in chronic (3C, 3D) respiratory alkalosis.	Looks like partially compensated respiratory alkalosis as for 20 mm fall in $PaCO_2$ the pH has gone up by 0.1 from 7.4 or the rise in pH is 0.05 for 10 mm change in $PaCO_2$.
4.	HCO_3 has fallen by 1.5 for a $PaCO_2$ fall of 10	If it is pure respiratory alkalosis the HCO_3 should have fallen by 2.5 to 5 for a 10 mm fall in $PaCO_2$ (4E, 4F).
5.	Is this ABG reading correct?	pH of 7.5 corresponds to H^+ of 30 (see chapter 7 on the pH). In this case calculated $H^+ = 24 \times PaCO_2 / HCO_3$ i.e. $24 \times 20/22 = 21.8$ only. Therefore, this ABG report is not correct.

Diagnosis: Wrong ABG Report

If the report is not fully evaluated and only the pH and the $PaCO_2$ are taken into consideration, then the report would have been passed as a partially compensated respiratory alkalosis. If the $PaCO_2$ and HCO_3 readings are correct then the pH would be 7.68 or so and if the pH and HCO_3 are correct the $PaCO_2$ should have been 32 (all calculated by the formula $H^+ = 24 \times PaCO_2/HCO_3$)

Section III

Exercises

Exercise A

Now attempt to solve the following exercises on your own without the help from the book. Answers and explanations are on the next page.

Analyze these ABG Reports:

Ex 1	:	pH 7.28	PCO_2 60	HCO_3 27
Ex 2	:	pH 7.28	PCO_2 84	HCO_3 39
Ex 3	:	pH 7.3	PCO_2 30	HCO_3 15
Ex 4	:	pH 7.54	PCO_2 25	HCO_3 21
Ex 5	:	pH 7.46	PCO_2 20	HCO_3 15
Ex 6	:	pH 7.56	PCO_2 55	HCO_3 45
Ex 7	:	pH 7.2	PCO_2 80	HCO_3 32
Ex 8	:	pH 7.2	PCO_2 50	HCO_3 19
Ex 9	:	pH 7.45	PCO_2 70	HCO_3 50
Ex 10	:	pH 7.35	PCO_2 50	HCO_3 28
Ex 11	:	pH 7.38	PCO_2 39	HCO_3 24
Ex 12	:	pH 7.6	PCO_2 35	HCO_3 32
Ex 13	:	ABG from a 24 year old healthy female		
		pH 7.4	PCO_2 28	HCO_3 16
Ex 14	:	pH 7.5	PCO_2 20	HCO_3 22

ANSWERS TO EXERCISE A

Analyze the Following ABG Reports: Answers:

Ex 1 : pH 7.28 PCO_2 60 HCO_3 27

Diagnosis: Pure acute respiratory acidosis.

Ex 2 : pH 7.28 PCO_2 84 HCO_3 39

Diagnosis: Pure chronic respiratory acidosis.

Ex 3 : pH 7.3 PCO_2 30 HCO_3 15

Diagnosis: Pure metabolic acidosis.

Ex 4 : pH 7.54 PCO_2 25 HCO_3 21

Diagnosis: Pure acute respiratory alkalosis.

Ex 5 : pH 7.46 PCO_2 20 HCO_3 15

Diagnosis: Pure chronic respiratory alkalosis.

Ex 6 : pH 7.56 PCO_2 55 HCO_3 45

Diagnosis: Pure metabolic alkalosis.

Ex7 : pH 7.2 PCO_2 80 HCO_3 32

Diagnosis : Acute -on-chronic respiratory acidosis

Or

Partially compensated acute respiratory acidosis.

Ex 8 : pH 7.2 PCO_2 50 HCO_3 19

Diagnosis: Mixed disorder with respiratory acidosis and metabolic acidosis.

E × 9 : pH 7.45 PCO_2 70 HCO_3 50

Diagnosis: Mixed disorder with respiratory acidosis and metabolic alkalosis.

Ex 10 : pH 7.35 PCO_2 50 HCO_3 28

Diagnosis: Compensated respiratory acidosis.

Ex 11 : pH 7.38 PCO_2 39 HCO_3 24

Diagnosis: No evidence of an acid base disorder on the ABG analysis. Correlate clinically.

Ex 12 : pH 7.6 PCO_2 35 HCO_3 32

Diagnosis: Mixed disorder with respiratory alkalosis and metabolic alkalosis.

Ex13 ABG from a 24 year old healthy female

pH 7.4 PCO_2 28 HCO_3 16

Diagnosis: Normal ABG in a pregnant female.

Ex 14 : pH 7.5 PCO_2 20 HCO_3 22

Diagnosis: Wrong ABG report.

If this report is not fully evaluated and only the pH and the $PaCO_2$ are taken into consideration, then the report would have been passed as a partially compensated respiratory alkalosis. If the PCO_2 and HCO_3 readings are correct then the pH should be 7.68 or so; and if the pH and HCO_3 are correct the PCO_2 should be 32. (All calculated by the formula $H^+ = 24 \times PaCO_2/HCO_3$).

For detailed explanations see the corresponding exercise numbers on the previous pages.

Exercise B

S No.	*pH*	*PCO_2*	*HCO_3*	*Acid base disorder is.....*
1.	7.3	30	14	
2.	7.5	20	14	
3.	7.6	20	17	
4.	7.6	30	28	
5.	7.5	50	36	
6.	7.45	80	54	
7.	7.3	80	37	
8.	7.23	75	30	
9.	7.4	40	24	
10.	7.25	63	26	
11.	7.25	45	19	
12.	7.38	12	24	

Answers to Exercise B

S No	*pH*	*PCO_2*	*HCO_3*	*Acid base disorder is.....*
1.	7.3	30	14	Metabolic acidosis
2.	7.5	20	14	Chronic respiratory alkalosis
3.	7.6	20	17	Acute respiratory alkalosis
4.	7.6	30	28	Acute respiratory alkalosis and Metabolic alkalosis
5.	7.5	50	36	Metabolic alkalosis
6.	7.45	80	54	Metabolic alkalosis and Chronic respiratory acidosis
7.	7.3	80	37	Chronic respiratory acidosis
8.	7.23	75	30	Acute on chronic respiratory acidosis or partially compensated acute respiratory acidosis
9.	7.4	40	24	Normal ABG report. Correlate clinically
10.	7.25	63	26	Acute respiratory acidosis
11.	7.25	45	19	Respiratory and metabolic acidosis
12.	7.38	12	24	Wrong report. pH and HCO_3 are normal. PCO_2 can not be 12.

Exercise C

Identify possible acid base disorders in the following cases –

1. JD, a 68 year old man with chronic obstructive pulmonary disease and chronic renal failure presented to the emergency room. An arterial blood gas reading on admission, breathing room air was as follows -

   pH 7.22 PCO_2 52 PaO_2 50 HCO_3 20 SaO_2 82%
2. TM, a 36 year old AIDS patient admitted with an altered mental state. Room air ABGs were as follows

   pH 7.15 PCO_2 36 PaO_2 70 HCO_3 12 SaO_2 86%
3. DN, a 45 year old cirrhotic admitted with vomiting for three days and altered mental status. Room air blood gases were -

   pH 7.56 PCO_2 36 PaO_2 98 HCO_3 27 SaO_2 96%
4. BN, a 25 year old female patient admitted with dyspnea for six hours. Room air ABGs showed -

   pH 7.6 PCO_2 30 PaO_2 106 HCO_3 28 SaO_2 99%
5. HS, a 68 year old patient who has been a heavy smoker all his life presents with the following ABGs -

   pH 7.36 PCO_2 50 PaO_2 78 HCO_3 28 SaO_2 88%
6. TE, a 62 year old with cor pulmonale came to the ER with complaints of cough and phlegm. Room air ABGs showed -

   pH 7.24 PCO_2 78 PaO_2 68 HCO_3 32 SaO_2 80%
7. A patient with 'acute exacerbation of COPD' had to be intubated for respiratory failure. Immediate post intubation ABGs showed -

   pH 7.15 PCO_2 56 PaO_2 268 HCO_3 18 SaO_2 99.9%

8. HD, a 28 year old female being treated for anxiety disorder presented to the ER. An ABG was done as the oxygen saturation was low on pulse oximetry. The report was -

   pH 7.58 PCO_2 22 PaO_2 54 HCO_3 20 SaO_2 70%

9. TG, a 44 year old asthmatic patient who continues to smoke four cigarettes a day was admitted for surgical removal of an ovarian mass. The ABG showed -

   pH 7.44 PCO_2 22 PaO_2 58 HCO_3 14 SaO_2 72 %

10. MN, a 68 year old patient came to the ER on a cold December morning complaining of headache every morning. His wife living with him has similar symptoms for the same duration. An ABG showed -

    pH 7.44 PCO_2 37 PaO_2 86 HCO_3 23 SaO_2 97 % (calculated).

What will you do next?

ANSWERS TO EXERCISE C

1. Mixed disorder - Respiratory and metabolic acidosis.
2. Mixed disorder - Metabolic and respiratory acidosis.
3. Mixed disorder - Respiratory and metabolic alkalosis.
4. Mixed disorder - Respiratory and metabolic alkalosis.
5. Compensated chronic respiratory acidosis.
6. Partially compensated respiratory acidosis.
7. Mixed disorder - Metabolic and respiratory acidosis.
8. Acute respiratory alkalosis.
9. Chronic respiratory alkalosis
10. Probably carbon monoxide poisoning in an old person who has been trying to keep warm by heating his room with fire from coal or wood with inadequate ventilation in the room. Immediately order measured SaO_2 and an estimation of carboxyhemoglobin.

Do not try to diagnose blood gas disorder based solely on clinical associations

Remember, **not to diagnose the ABG by clinical associations alone**. For example, a patient with AIDS can be short of breath with respiratory alkalosis not only because of pneumocystis carinii (PCP) pneumonia but also because of hysteric hyperventilation, bronchial asthma or pulmonary embolism. He can also have respiratory acidosis from a drug overdose or metabolic acidosis from septicemia or kidney failure. There can be any number of combinations of disorders of the blood gas parameters.

Exercise D

1. PL, an 82 year old man with congestive heart failure was admitted with early pneumonia. Patient was on lasix, digoxin and coumadin. Admission ABG included

   pH 7.6 H^+ 24 PCO_2 35 PaO_2 56 HCO_3 32
   SaO_2 70%

2. HY, a 32 year old pregnant female with hyperemesis presented with tingling in both hands. Room air ABG showed -

   pH 7.5 H^+ 30 PCO_2 50 PaO_2 96 HCO_3 37
   SaO_2 98%

3. WT, a 27 year old asthmatic patient admitted to the hospital with shortness of breath. Admission ABGs were -

   pH 7.4 H^+ 40 PCO_2 30 PaO_2 76 HCO_3 18
   SaO_2 88 %

4. Patient WT in the above exercise no.3 continued to have low saturation on pulse oximeter. ABG on 5 L/ minute O_2 by nasal cannula now shows -

   pH 7.4 H^+ 40 PCO_2 48 PaO_2 52 HCO_3 26
   SaO_2 68 %

5. Patient WT in the above exercise placed on 50% ventimask with only minimal improvement in saturation. The patient also appeared lethargic. ABG showed -

   pH 7.28 H^+ 54 PCO_2 54 PaO_2 62 HCO_3 24
   SaO_2 74 %

6. Above patient WT was intubated and put on 100 percent O_2 (FiO_2 = 1.0). The blood gas few hours later showed -

   pH 7.5 H^+ 30 PCO_2 24 PaO_2 362 HCO_3 19
   SaO_2 99.9 %

7. BE, a 28 year old female patient under treatment for anxiety disorder presented to the ER after an argument with her employer. She complained of spasms in both her hands. The ABG showed -
   pH 7.52 H^+28 PCO_2 25 PaO_2 112 HCO_3 20
   SaO_2 99.9 %
8. RI, a 78 year old patient with COPD, corpulmonale came to the ER with history of shortness of breath and yellow phlegm. He was on digoxin and metalazone for the congestive heart failure and was waiting in the triage area for an hour. The ABG while breathing room air showed -
   pH 7.32 H^+ 48 PCO_2 56 PaO_2 172 HCO_3 32
   SaO_2 91%
9. SR, a 32 year old patient with history of recurrent admissions for drug overdoses came to the ER with altered mental status. ABG on room air showed -
   pH 7.1 H^+ 80 PCO_2 66 PaO_2 62 HCO_3 20
   SaO_2 78 %
10. GT, an 86 year old person living alone found to be confused by the emergency medical services brought to the ER. Patient was discharged after (PTCA) percutaneous transluminal coronary angioplasty three months ago. He now complains of severe chest pains which occur at rest and are relieved by sublingual nitrate tablets. He looks comfortable and is in no apparent distress.
    pH 7.28 H^+ 54 PCO_2 58 PaO_2 62 HCO_3 26
    SaO_2 78 %

ANSWERS TO EXERCISE D

1. Mixed metabolic and respiratory alkalosis with hypoxia.
2. Pure metabolic alkalosis.
3. Acute respiratory alkalosis.
4. Acute respiratory acidosis superimposed on respiratory alkalosis leading to a normal pH with raised PCO_2. This is a danger sign in an asthmatic.
5. Acute respiratory acidosis in an asthmatic secondary to respiratory failure due to respiratory muscle fatigue. This patient may soon need respiratory support.
6. Acute respiratory alkalosis secondary to hyperventilation on the ventilator. If the patient's respiratory rate is high, the ventilator (in assist control mode) will be repeatedly triggered causing hyperventilation. (See book on ventilators by the same author).
7. Respiratory alkalosis due to hyperventilation.
8. Wrong report. The PaO_2 while breathing room air cannot be 172.
9. Mixed respiratory and metabolic acidosis.
10. Methemoglobinemia due to excess nitrate ingestion. There is also respiratory acidosis. Almost 50 % PTCA re-stenose in the first 6 months. This patient was using excessive nitrates to relieve his anginal pain.

Exercise E

Calculate the alveolo-arterial oxygen gradient for the following patients who live at the sea port of Dover.

Q.	pH	PCO_2	HCO_3	PaO_2	FiO_2	A-aDO_2
1.	7.3	30	14	80	Room Air	
2.	7.5	20	14	440	1.0	
3.	7.6	20	17	120	Room Air	
4.	7.6	30	28	200	0.4	
5.	7.5	50	36	130	0.3	
6.	7.45	80	54	100	0.4	
7.	7.3	80	37	70	0.4	
8.	7.23	75	30	80	0.5	
9.	7.4	40	24	90	0.3	
10.	7.25	63	26	320	0.6	

Answers to Exercise E

Q.	pH	PCO_2	HCO_3	PaO_2	FiO_2	$AaDO_2$
1.	7.3	30	14	80	Room Air	32
	$(760 - 47) \times 0.21 - 80 - 30 - 30/4 = 32$					
2.	7.5	20	14	440	1.0	248
	$(760 - 47) \times 1.0 - 440 - 20 - 20/4 = 248$					
	Remember, that at very high FiO_2 values this formula does not apply very accurately. Purpose of this exercise is to make you understand the principle of calculating A-a gradient (A-aDO_2).					
3.	7.6	20	17	120	Room Air	5
4.	7.6	30	28	200	0.4	48
	$(760 - 47) \times 0.4 - 200 - 30 - 30/4 = 47$					
5.	7.5	50	36	130	0.3	21
	$(760 - 47) \times 0.3 - 130 - 50 - 50/4 = 21$					
6.	7.45	80	54	100	0.4	85
7.	7.3	80	37	70	0.4	115
8.	7.23	75	30	80	0.5	183
9.	7.4	40	24	90	0.3	74
10.	7.25	63	26	320	0.6	29

Exercise F

Calculate the oxygen content of the whole blood (CaO_2) in the following cases -

S. No	*pH*	*PCO_2*	*HCO_3*	*PaO_2*	*Hb gm %*	*Atmospheric pressure*	*SaO_2*	*CaO_2*
1.	7.3	30	14	90	14	1.0	97	
2.	7.5	20	14	70	12	1.0	92	
3.	7.6	20	17	900	15	2.0	99.9	
4.	7.6	30	28	900	10	2.0	99.9	
5.	7.5	50	36	800	15	1.5	70	
6.	7.45	80	54	100	14	1.0	99	
7.	7.3	80	37	80	16	1.0	94	
8.	7.23	75	30	70	16	1.0	91	
9.	7.4	40	24	50	12	1.0	70	
10.	7.25	63	26	60	14	1.0	82	

ANSWERS TO EXERCISE F

S. No	*pH*	*PCO_2*	*HCO_3*	*PaO_2*	*Hb gm %*	*Atmospheric pressure*	*SaO_2*	*CaO_2*
1.	7.3	30	14	90	14	1.0	97	18.4

$(14 \times 1.34 \times 0.97) + 0.003 \times 90 = 18.19 + 0.27 = 18.46$

2.	7.5	20	14	70	12	1.0	92	15.0

$(12 \times 1.34 \times 0.92) + 0.003 \times 70 = 14.79 + 0.21 = 15.0$

3.	7.6	20	17	900	15	2.0	99.9	22.7

$(15 \times 1.34 \times 0.999) + 0.003 \times 900 = 20.08 + 2.7 = 22.7$

Note the significant contribution made by the O_2 dissolved in the plasma i.e. 2.7 ml

4.	7.6	30	28	900	10	2.0	99.9	16.08

$(10 \times 1.34 \times 0.99) + 0.003 \times 900 = 13.38 + 2.7 = 13.38$

5.	7.5	50	36	800	15	1.5	70	16.47

$(15 \times 1.34 \times 0.7) + 0.003 \times 800 = 14.07 + 2.4 = 16.47$

Compare this with exercise F1 above. Note that low oxygen content carried by the hemoglobin (14.07 compared to 18.19) is counterbalanced by increasing the oxygen dissolved in the plasma (2.4 ml compared to 0.27 ml in exercise F1) by increasing the atmospheric pressure. If high FiO_2 is added, much more dissolved oxygen can be carried in the plasma. This principle is used in the treatment of carbon monoxide poisoning.

6.	7.45	80	54	100	14	1.0	99	18.87

$(14 \times 1.34 \times 0.99) + 0.003 \times 100 = 18.57 + 0.3 = 18.87$

7.	7.3	80	37	80	16	1.0	94	20.3

$(16 \times 1.34 \times 0.94) + 0.003 \times 80 = 20.1 + 0.24 = 20.3$

8.	7.23	75	30	70	16	1.0	91	19.7

$(16\times 1.34 \times 0.91) + 0.003 \times 50 = 19.51 + 0.15 = 11.4$

9.	7.4	40	24	50	12	1.0	70	11.4

$(12 \times 1.34 \times 0.7) + 0.003 \times 50 = 11.25 + 0.15 = 11.4$

10.	7.25	63	26	60	14	1.0	82	15.6

$(14 \times 1.34 \times 0.82) + 0.003 \times 60 = 15.4 + 0.18 = 15.58$

Exercise G

Match the following clinical conditions (1 to 15) with the corresponding blood gas reports (A to O). Choose the **most appropriate** answer –

1. Salicylate poisoning
2. Cardiac arrest
3. Ventilator malfunction
4. Alcohol intoxication
5. Drug overdose, no loss of consciousness
6. Alcohol intake followed by blindness
7. Some alcohol intake followed by acute renal failure
8. Opium overdose with loss of consciousness and aspiration
9. Bronchial asthma
10. Sepsis
11. Status epilepticus
12. Diarrhea
13. Diuretics
14. Addison's disease
15. Cushing's syndrome

Match the above questions with these answers –

A. Respiratory acidosis and metabolic acidosis
B. Respiratory alkalosis and metabolic acidosis with anion gap
C. Respiratory acidosis with no A-a gradient
D. Respiratory acidosis with A-a gradient
E. High anion gap metabolic acidosis & osmolal gap
F. High osmolal gap
G. Metabolic acidosis

H. Respiratory alkalosis or respiratory acidosis
I. Metabolic acidosis or metabolic alkalosis
J. Metabolic alkalosis, hypokalemia, high urine chloride
K. Metabolic acidosis and hypokalemia
L. Metabolic acidosis with hyperkalemia
M. Metabolic alkalosis, hypokalemia, high urine chloride
N. Respiratory acidosis, metabolic acidosis, myocardial infarction
O. Respiratory acidosis or alkalosis, low peak expiratory flow rate

ANSWERS TO EXERCISE G

1. Salicylate poisoning B
2. Cardiac arrest N
3. Ventilator malfunction H
4. Alcohol intoxication E
5. Drug overdose, no loss of consciousness C
6. Alcohol intake followed by blindness E
7. Some alcohol intake followed by acute renal failure F
8. Opium overdose with loss of consciousness and aspiration D
9. Bronchial asthma O
10. Sepsis G, I
11. Status epilepticus A
12. Diarrhea K
13. Diuretics J
14. Addison's disease L
15. Cushing's syndrome M

In the above exercise more than one answer can be correct. Emphasis is placed on the **most appropriate** answer. Cardiac arrest causes metabolic acidosis but it can also lead to respiratory arrest. Similarly seizures cause metabolic acidosis but prolonged attack can be associated with respiratory failure (transient) with or without aspiration.

Space available here and the scope of this book does not permit a full discussion of the above disorders. For that refer to a text book of medicine. You may also refer to 'Fluids And Electrolytes Made Easy' by the same author.

Remember

While looking at the ABG report always consider the clinical picture and determine the following—

1. Is the patient hypoxic?
2. What is the FiO_2?
3. Is the PaO_2 appropriate for the given FiO_2?
4. What is the alveolo arterial gradient?
5. What is the relation of the PaO_2 to SaO_2 and SpO_2?
6. Is the oxygen content of blood adequate to prevent hypoxia at the tissue level?
7. Is the patient hypoventilating / hyperventilating or ventilating normally for his CO_2 production?

Also Remember

While analyzing an acid base disorder determine the following—

1. The disorder is pure or mixed.
2. The disorder is respiratory or metabolic.
3. The disorder is acute or chronic, if respiratory.
4. If metabolic acidosis, what is the anion gap.
5. If metabolic acidosis/suspected alcohol consumption determine what is the calculated and measured osmolality, osmolal gap and gap-gap.
6. If metabolic alkalosis then is it chloride responsive i.e. what is the urine chloride.
7. Does the H^+ ion concentration correspond to the PCO_2 and the HCO_3 ratio?
8. If the clinical picture of the patient does not correlate with the ABG report do not hesitate to repeat it before taking drastic measures like intubation!

Section IV

Summary

Read

What is obvious on the ABG report

1. SaO_2
2. HCO_3 *and BE*
3. PaO_2
4. $PaCO_2$
5. pH

MUST read

What is not obvious on the ABG report

6. $A\text{-}aDO_2$

A-a Gradient

$$A\text{-}a\ DO_2 = PaO_2 - PaCO_2 - \frac{PaCO_2}{4}$$

PaO_2 v/s SaO_2

PaO_2	SaO_2
40	75
55	88
59	89
60	90
80	95
100	97
140	99
150	99.9

PULSE OXIMETRY

$$SpO_2 = \frac{\text{Oxy Hb}}{\text{OxyHb+DeoxyHb}} \times 100$$

$$SpO_2 = \frac{\text{Oxy Hb}}{\text{Oxy Hb + Deoxy Hb + CO Hb + Meth Hb}} \times 100$$

Partial Pressure of a Gas

Partial pressure of a gas = Atmospheric pressure (dry) × Fraction of that gas in atmosphere

PiO_2 = *(760 - Water vapor pressure)* × *0.21*

At sea level water vapor pressure is 47

$$PiO_2 = 760 - 47 \times 0.21$$
$$= 713 \times 0.21$$
$$= 150$$

Oxygen Content of Whole Blood - CaO_2

$$CaO_2 = (Hb \times 1.34 \times SaO_2) + 0.003 \times PaO_2$$

e.g. $(14 \times 1.34 \times 0.99) + 0.003 \times 100$

= 18.57 + 0.3 = 18.87 ml

Remember About $PaCO_2$

Respiratory rate alone does not tell about hypoventilation or hyperventilation

In patients prone to retain carbon dioxide start oxygen in lowest possible concentrations with a close watch on PaO_2, $PaCO_2$ and breathing pattern

pH

$$pH = Constant\ K \times \frac{log\ PaCO_2}{log\ HCO_3}$$

(pH is negative log of H^+ concentration)

Relation of pH to H^+ ion concentration

1. $H^+ = K \times \frac{PaCO_2}{HCO_3}$

(K is a constant with a value of 24)

$$= 24 \times \frac{PaCO_2}{HCO_3}$$

2. Change in pH by 0.1 = Change in H^+ ion concentration by 20%

Change in pH vs Change in H^+ Concentration

Change in pH by 0.1 = Change in H^+ concentration by 20%

pH	H^+ ion concentration
7.0	100
7.1	80
7.2	64
7.3	50
7.4	40
7.5	30
7.6	24
7.7	20

NORMAL RANGES

	Normal Range	*Mean*
pH	7.35 to 7.45	7.40
$PaCO_2$	*35 to 45*	*40*
HCO_3	*22 to 28*	*24*

pH of 7.4 corresponds to H^+ of 40 nmol

pH less than 7.35 means acidosis

pH more than 7.45 means alkalosis

pH	*Acidosis/ Alkalosis*	*$PaCO_2$*	*HCO_3*	*Disorder*
Decreased	Acidosis	Increased	Increased	**Respiratory acidosis**
Decreased	Acidosis	Decreased	Decreased	**Metabolic acidosis**
Increased	Alkalosis	Increased	Increased	**Metabolic alkalosis**
Increased	Alkalosis	Decreased	Decreased	**Respiratory alkalosis**

METABOLIC ACIDOSIS

If Metabolic Acidosis - Look for Anion Gap

1. AGMA - Anion gap is high
2. NAGMA - Normal anion gap

ANION GAP

ANION GAP is an In-vitro phenomenon
(In real life there is no anion gap)

$$ANION \quad GAP = Na - (Cl + HCO_3)$$

Causes of high Anion Gap

1. Endogenous anions
2. Exogenous anions

If Anion Gap Metabolic Acidosis (AGMA)
Look for Osmolal Gap

Osmolal gap = Measured Osmolality - Calculated Osmolality

Measured osmolality = Calculated osmolality + Osmolality due to other osmotically active substances like alcohols or mannitol

$$\text{Calculated osmolality} = 2\,Na + \frac{Glucose}{18} + \frac{BUN}{2.8}$$

If Anion Gap Metabolic Acidosis (AGMA)
Look for Gap-Gap

		Change in anion		Change in
Gap - Gap	=	gap from	/	HCO_3 from
		mean (12)		mean (25)

AGMA OR ANION GAP METABOLIC ACIDOSIS

ANION GAP

ANION GAP is an In-vitro phenomenon

(In real life there is no anion gap)

$$ANION\ \ GAP = Na - (Cl + HCO_3)$$

Causes of high Anion Gap

1. Endogenous anions
2. Exogenous anions

Important Endogenous Sources of Anions Include

	Cause		*Anion accumulated*
1.	Cardiopulmonary failure	-	Lactate
2.	Renal failure	-	Organic acids, SO_4, PO_4
3.	Diabetes Mellitus	-	Keto acids
4.	Starvation	-	Keto acids
5.	Anaerobic metabolism in cases of seizures or sepsis	-	Lactate

Important Exogenous Sources of Anions Include

	Cause		*Anion accumulated*
1.	Salicylates	-	Salicylic acid
2.	Ethanol	-	Keto and lactic acid
3.	Methanol	-	Formic acid
4.	Ethylene glycol	-	Glycolic and oxalic acid
5.	Paraldehyde		

Common Alcohols

Ethanol	:	Drinking alcohol
Methanol	:	Industrial alcohol
Ethylene glycol	:	Wind shield fluid or antifreeze in cars
Isopropyl alcohol	:	Rubbing alcohol used in hospitals

Common Poisonings and Anion Gap and Serum Osmolality		
	Anion Gap	*Serum Osmolality*
Salicylates*	Increased	Not increased
Isopropyl alcohol	Not increased	Increased
Ethanol	Increased	increased

Salicylates* - Present in many over the counter analgesics

How to Remember

Causes of Increased Anion Gap

D	Diabetic keto-acidosis
A	Alcohol
R	Renal failure
L	Lactic acidosis from any cause
I	Iron poisoning
N	No food (starvation)
G	Generalized seizures
S	Sepsis
A	Aspirin poisoning
R	Rhabdomyolysis
E	Ethylene glycol
I	INH
M	Methanol
P	Paraldehyde

NAGMA or Non-anion Gap Metabolic Acidosis

Non Anion Gap Metabolic Acidosis

(Rise in chloride compensates for HCO_3 loss)

Sites of Bicarbonate loss

1. Gastrointestinal
2. Urinary

Causes of Gastrointestinal HCO_3 Loss

- Diarrhea
- Small bowel fistula
- Ileostomy
- Ureterosigmoidostomy
- Ileal ureter

Causes of Urinary HCO_3 Loss

- Renal tubular acidosis
- Acetazolamide therapy
- Chronic urinary obstruction

Usual Picture in Various Types of Renal Tubular Acidosis

	Urine pH	*Serum K^+*
Distal (RTA I)	> 5.5	Low
Proximal (RTAII)	< 5.5	Low
RTA IV	<5.5	High

METABOLIC ALKALOSIS

If Metabolic Alkalosis Look for Urine Chloride

Urine chloride <15 meq/l	-	chloride responsive
Urine chloride > 15 meq/l	-	chloride resistant (Exception – diuretics)

Chloride Responsive Metabolic Alkalosis

- Vomiting
- Continuous nasogastric aspiration
- Volume contracted states
- Diuretics

Chloride Resistant Metabolic Alkalosis

- Hypercortisolism
- Hyperaldosteronism
- Sodium bicarbonate therapy
- Severe renal artery stenosis

REMEMBER

While looking at the ABG report always consider the clinical picture and determine the following

1. Is the patient hypoxic?
2. What is the FiO_2?
3. Is the PaO_2 appropriate for the given FiO_2?
4. What is the alveolo-arterial gradient?
5. What is the relation of the PaO_2 to SaO_2 and SpO_2?
6. Is the oxygen content of blood adequate to prevent hypoxia at the tissue level?
7. Is the patient hypoventilating/hyperventilating or ventilating normally for his CO_2 production?

While analyzing an acid base disorder

Determine the Following

1. The disorder is pure or mixed.
2. The disorder is respiratory or metabolic.
3. The disorder is acute or chronic, if respiratory.
4. If metabolic acidosis, what is the anion gap.
5. If metabolic alkalosis then is it chloride responsive i.e. what is the urine chloride.
6. Does the H^+ ion concentration correspond to the PCO_2 and the HCO_3 ratio?
7. **If the clinical picture of the patient does not correlate with the ABG do not hesitate to repeat it before taking drastic measures like intubation!**

References

Anup A. B., *Arterial Blood Gas Analysis Made Easy* (1996) ISBN 0965708373, First Edition, Anup Publishing, USA.

Kumar P. J. & Clark L. C. (1990) in *Clinical Medicine*, Acid-Base hemostasis, Physiologic Principles, Second Edition 1990, Pg 502 Bailliere Tindall, W. B. Saunders, UK.

Marino P. L. (1991) Mixed Metabolic Acidosis, Pg 423-424 in *The ICU book*, Lea and Febiger, USA.

Weinberger S. E., Drazen J. M.00 (1994) Measurement of Gas Exchange, Arterial Blood Gases, Page 1156-1157 in *Harrison's Principles of Internal Medicine, Thirteenth Edition*, McGRAW Inc. USA.

Index